YEADON'S REGISTER

of

L N E R

LOCOMOTIVES

Volume Twenty- Seven

Class N 7
The GER & LNER 0-6-2T's

i

YEADON'S REGISTER OF L.N.E.R. LOCOMOTIVES - VOLUME 27

Dedicated to Annie Yeadon - *a lady in every sense of the word.*

EDITOR'S NOTE & ACKNOWLEDGEMENTS

Returning to a more manageable size, this volume features the history of one of the more popular LNER tank engines, the N7's.

The Great Eastern Railway was responsible for a fair number of enduring locomotive designs spanning the requirements of any railway be they tank engine, tender engine, goods or passenger type and, towards the end of its existence Stratford produced an 0-6-2 tank engine design which was to serve both the LNER and British Railways until overtaken by electrification.

Ongoing development of the GER design by the LNER between 1925 and 1928 eventually split the class into four distinctive Parts with further alterations taking place in later years to the original Stratford built engines and the Part 1 engines. Of the eventual total of 134 locomotives within N7 class, Stratford had built only twenty-two, the balance being supplied by two outside contractors and two other LNER works. However, Stratford became responsible for the maintenance of the whole class from introduction to demise which in itself was something of a record.

Perhaps it was inevitable that a representative of Class N7 would be preserved, though not for the National Collection but nevertheless an example exists today in working order and resident in that area of the former Great Eastern territory in which the class worked.

The plethora of information contained within *Yeadon's Register* needs careful checking before publication and Eric Fry has taken on the role of 'proof reader' for this gigantic task. It is seemingly a thankless and daunting task but Eric finds great satisfaction checking the numbers, facts, figures and illustrations which go to make up each volume of this monumental work. Once again, thank you Eric for a task well done.

The staff at Hull University Archive continue to make everything accessible to us as usual and manage to do it with a smile each time - thanks.

Typesetting numbers is no easy job as any 'setter' will tell you but to do it with any degree of accuracy demands concentration and dedication. So, thanks to Mike and Tina for their continued dedication to 'getting it right'. Amadeus Press continue to carry out their part in this ongoing 'work' with the professionalism served up with each volume.

As this volume went to press, word reached us that WBY's widow Annie had passed away aged 95. A lady of patience and understanding, amongst other qualities, Annie Yeadon was a friend and benefactor to this series. We pass on our sympathy to Jean and Simon for their sad loss but on the other hand we must thank them for their continued support.

The next *Yeadon's Register of LNER Locomotives*, Volume 28, contains the repair history of some of the larger LNER tank engines found within classes R1, S1, T1 and the former WM&CQ singleton 0-8-2T.

The Yeadon Collection is available for inspection and anyone who wishes to inspect it should contact:-
The Archivist
Brynmor Jones Library
University of Hull
Hull
HU6 7RX
Tel: 01482-465265
A catalogue of the Yeadon collection is available.

First published in the United Kingdom by
BOOK LAW PUBLICATIONS 2003 in association with CHALLENGER
382 Carlton Hill, Nottingham, NG4 1JA.
Printed and bound by The Amadeus Press, Cleckheaton, West Yorkshire.

ii

INTRODUCTION

Introduced by the Great Eastern Railway in 1915, the GER Class L77 was to become one of the most useful medium sized tank engines owned by the LNER who classified them N7.

At first only two engines were built, one with a saturated boiler, No.1000 (actually ex works 31st December 1914) and the other, No.1001 with a superheated boiler. The 12-element superheater did not give a great advantage over the saturated boiler. No more of these 0-6-2 tanks were built until 1921 when Stratford turned out ten more, all with saturated boilers for use on the passenger services out of Liverpool Street.

The next batch of N7's was also built at Stratford but this time under the auspices of the LNER. These ten engines, delivered during 1923 and 1924, were basically the same as the GER period engines except that they were fitted, from new, with superheated boilers, but with eighteen elements instead of the twelve used on No.1001.

The LNER decided to build another 112 N7's giving them Group Standard status and these were built during the years up to 1928 by the LNER workshops at Gorton and Doncaster and also by two outside contractors. Whereas the Stratford built engines had right hand drive, these were all made with left hand drive also the overall height was cut down to give them greater route availability mainly, in the first instance, access to the Metropolitan Widened Lines.

In 1925 Gorton works supplied the first lot of Group Standard N7's, all ten numbered in the 4XX series. These were followed by another twenty from Gorton, numbered in the 8XX range, delivered between January 1926 and February 1927. Meanwhile, R. Stephenson & Co. built the twenty 9XX series engines between October 1925 and January 1926. All fifty of the 1925 to 1927 built engines became class Part 1, whilst the twenty-two Stratford built N7's, both saturated and superheated types became N7/GE.

During 1927 and 1928 thirty more N7's were delivered, twenty from W. Beardmore & Co. (Nos.2642 to 2661) followed by ten from Gorton (Nos.2632 to 2641). Like the previous fifty, these engines were built to fit the Metropolitan load gauge, had left-hand drive, Belpaire fireboxes but had long travel valves rather than short travel valves. These became Class N7 Part 2.

Coincidental with the construction of the Gorton batch, Doncaster was busy constructing thirty-two more N7's which were noticeably different from previous examples in having a round-topped firebox. They also had long travel valves. These final thirty-two (Nos.2600 to 2631) became Class Part 3.

The Diagram issued for the first type of N7 boiler was number 30, be they superheated or saturated examples. Eleven of this Diagram were built saturated with the other eleven superheated; all were used on N7/GE. The next Diagram was 98, issued to the LNER Group Standard boiler with Belpaire firebox, and was an updated version of Diagram 30. Diagram 98 boilers consisted of a one ring 4ft 8in. diameter barrel whilst the Diagram 30 boiler barrel consisted of two rings, the front one being 4ft 9in. outside diameter and the rear portion 4ft 8in. outside diameter. Boiler Nos.980 to 989, used on the 400 series engines when new, had GC (Gorton) type circular firehole door. All other Diagram 98 boiler types, including the batch numbered 2005 to 2044 and used on the 800 and 900 series engines, had dished firehole doors of GN (Doncaster) origin. Further Diagram 98 boilers (2045-2054 and 2087-2106) were used initially on the engines consisting N7 Part 2. All Diagram 98 boilers had Ross 'pop' safety valves from new. Finally Diagram 101 was issued for the round-topped firebox boiler (Nos.2055-2086) introduced with the first of the Doncaster built (Part 3) engines. Except for the round-topped firebox, the boiler was essentially the same as the Diagram 98 version.

The first replacement boilers were constructed in 1928/9 when five Diagram 30 boilers became the last of that type. These five boilers were superheated and their building enabled the ten saturated boilers fitted to engines 8002 to 8011 to be fitted with 18-element superheaters and No.8001's boiler to be upgraded. The saturated boiler fitted to No.8000 was condemned in 1929 and the engine was fitted with a superheated boiler. These Diagram 30 replacements also has Ross 'pop' safety valves, the first Diagram 30 boilers so fitted, Ramsbottom being the standard on the earlier boilers; Ross 'pops' were eventually fitted to all the earlier boilers (except No.1000) during LNER days. In the 1930 to 1933 period ten more Diagram 98 boilers were made as replacements for the eighty then in use on the N7/1 and N7/2 engines. These ten boilers could also be used on the Stratford built engines because they were fitted with alternative feed arrangements via the back of the boiler and via the dome. In the event none were ever fitted to the N7/GE engines. During 1932 two more Diagram 101 boilers were built as spares for those fitted to the Part 3 engines. Five more were built in 1936 and it was this last boiler type which continued to be constructed and from 1940 it became the standard boiler for the class with all but two N7's eventually having the Diagram 101 type. The last example of the more than 170 Diagram 101 boilers was built as late as 1957. Between 1941 and 1957 a total of 135 Diagram 101 boilers were constructed.

See the accompanying tables on pages 7 to 10 for the full list of N7 boilers and their specific allocations.

Rebuilding of the GE built engines began in February 1940 and all got a round-topped firebox (Diagram 101) boiler but no other major changes occurred to this sub class and all twenty-two examples became N7 Part 4. Because of the urgent need to renew the boilers of the N7/GE engines and also because of the wartime conditions prevailing, it was decided to fit second-hand Diagram 101 boilers, some of which were nearing the end of their working lives too. In fact, only three received brand new boilers at the time of their rebuilding

The N7/1's were also treated to Diagram 101 boilers from May 1943 onwards and all of these became Part 5 engines, the last rebuild (No.69627 ex-460) taking place in September 1956. Like the N7/GE engines before them, the N7/1 had to make do with second-hand Diagram 101 boilers during the early wartime period.

Those N7/2 engines which received the Diagram 101 boiler joined the last thirty-two of the class as Part 3 engines. Only two N7's failed to get the round-topped firebox boiler and these were both N7/2's - 2649 (69689) and 2655 (69695). No.69689 was the first of the class to be condemned, just as the penultimate Diagram 101 boiler (No.24803) was being fitted to N7/5 No.69651 in March 1957.

1

Two engines, Nos.1000 and 1001 were built by the Great Eastern Railway at Stratford in December 1914 and February 1915 respectively. These two were to form the LNER Class N7 0-6-2T in 1923 but from 1915 until 1921 were the only examples built. Although both had mechanical lubricator and snifting valves, only No.1001 had a superheater, which was a 12-element Robinson type. Note the cab roof cut-out, a feature peculiar to these two, and which they lost whilst LNER. They also had the upper lamp iron on the top of the smokebox front plate. Later this was changed to a position on the door.

The twelve GE built engines were all fitted with Westinghouse brake and these N7's remained as such until withdrawal. Those engines built at LNER works and by R. Stephenson between December 1923 and December 1928, were fitted with both Westinghouse brake and vacuum ejector. However, the twenty engines supplied by Beardmore in 1927 came with steam brake and vacuum ejector.

Three of the Westinghouse engines were altered to steam brake by British Railways (for P&P working, *see* later) but a greater proportion (12) of the steam braked engines had been altered to Westinghouse brake by the LNER during the 1930's.

Eleven engines were equipped with push & pull gear in the BR period with five so done in 1949. Four more followed in 1951 but no more were done until a single example was fitted in 1954. Then, in May 1957, the final one was dealt with. Those done in 1949 were from the original batch of steam brake and vacuum ejector fitted N7's, whilst three of the four fitted in 1951 also came from this batch. So as to complete the order for the four P&P fitted engines, it was necessary to convert a Westinghouse fitted engine to steam brake and vacuum ejector in October 1951. Likewise, the 1954 and 1957 push & pull fitted engines were selected from Westinghouse engines as there were now no steam braked N7's.

All had been fitted from new with condensing apparatus but it was deemed unnecessary and between January 1935 and February 1938 all the N7's had their condensing gear removed.

The twelve Stratford built N7's in the GER 1000 number range were all renumbered by the LNER by having 7000 added. The ten built at Stratford during the early days of the LNER came out with the sectional suffix as Nos.990ᴇ to 999ᴇ, later becoming 7990 to 7999. The N7/1 engines took up random vacant numbers between 409 and 988. The N7/2's had the tidier number group 2632 to 2661 whilst the N7/3 engines carried 2600 to 2631.

In 1944 Nos.8000 to 8011 were renumbered, temporarily, 7978 to 7989 in order to allow diesel shunters to take up the 8000 series that they had been allocated in the 1943 Thompson renumbering scheme.

That particular scheme saw the number group 9600 to 9733 allocated to the N7 class. The numbers awarded were roughly though not strictly in order of building but certainly in order of the original class Parts:-

New Nos.	Old Nos.	Class Part.
9600-9621	7978-7999	N7/GE
9622-9651	409 to 873	N7/1
9652-9671	907 to 988	N7/1
9672-9681	2632-2641	N7/2
9682-9701	2642-2661	N7/2
9702-9733	2600-2631	N7/3

British Railways simply added 60000 to those numbers and all the class were so treated, however, before the fifth digit came into use a number of N7's carried the E prefix.

On their introduction the initial N7's went to work on the Enfield and Chingford lines. However, when the N7 class started to grow in quantity in 1921, the new members of the class began to take on the heavier and faster trains into and out of Liverpool Street and for this task they were allocated to Stratford. In fact the first twelve N7's, all built at Stratford by the GER, spent all of their working lives allocated to Stratford from introduction to withdrawal - quite a record involving in most cases forty years of continuous service in the area. Add to that the fact that all the repairs to those twelve GE-built engines were carried out at Stratford works and the realisation of the relationship between the Class N7 0-6-2T and Stratford is easily understood.

The majority of the first of the LNER built batches,

Eventually ten more engines of the same class, Nos.1002 to 1011, were built at Stratford between June and November 1921. All had snifting valves but were not superheated. They had a lower arch to cab roof but no cut-out over the entrance. Nos.1002, 1003 and 1004 only had the top lamp iron on the smokebox. No.1005 and all later ones had that iron fixed on the smokebox door. All ten had the dome 9in. further forward than on Nos. 1000 and 1001, and lubrication was by Detroit sight feed instead of mechanical.

Ten further engines, Nos.990E to 999E, were built at Stratford from 15th December 1923 to 19th March 1924. These all had superheater, and vacuum brake in addition to the Westinghouse for train braking. They also had a plain cast iron chimney instead of one with a brass rim. Until rebuilt from February 1940, with round top firebox, these twenty-two engines, Nos.7990 to 8011 were classed N7/GE.

Another ten N7's, randomly numbered in 409 to 475 series, were built at Gorton from 30th August to 11th December 1925. These were to the Metropolitan load gauge, had left hand drive but still with short travel valves. Safety valves were Ross 'pop' type instead of Ramsbottom and the boiler feed was through back plate injectors and not through the dome. The cab roof now had two full length rain strips and a hand grip was provided on the running plate adjacent to the front footstep.

(below) Twenty similar engines, this time randomly numbered in 907 to 988 series, were built by Robert Stephenson & Co., Darlington from 2nd October 1925 to 16th January 1926. Note that the buffers were still of GER pattern but some $1\frac{1}{4}$in. longer to match Group Standard draw hook. Nos.907, 912, 913, 916 and 919 began work on suburban trains into and out of King's Cross, and No.916, shedded at King's Cross, was fitted at the right hand front corner with the extra lamp irons for working on to the Southern Railway. No.912, also shedded at King's Cross, may have been so fitted, but none of the others were.

(opposite) Gorton then built another twenty similar engines, numbered in the 826 to 873 series, in the period from 19th January 1926 to 5th February 1927 and these were the last to have the short valve travel. These fifty became Part 1 of the class.

appearing from Stratford works in 1923 and 1924, were sent to varying locations on the ex-GN lines, some of which in the West Riding were well away from former GE territory. However, these Yorkshire based engines had all moved south to the London area within six months.

The ten Gorton built N7's of 1925, though initially allocated to depots at the southern end of the GN main line, had all moved to Stratford by 1928. The next batch from Gorton went mainly to Stratford though a few went direct to King's Cross. The twenty engines supplied by R. Stephenson during 1925 and 1926 also followed a similar course with the majority going to Stratford and others to either Hatfield, Hitchin or King's Cross. All of these contractor built engines went in the first instance to Gorton shed but they only stayed there for a couple of days for their acceptance trials. Gorton's third and final batch also ended up at Stratford by 1929 though their first shed had been Hatfield. Neasden shed also had a share of the R.Stephenson batch.

Stratford was eventually the main recipient of the twenty supplied by Beardmore & Co. in 1927, although in most cases King's Cross and Hatfield shed's kept hold of many of them for a good ten years before they went to the east London shed.

The thirty-two engines built by Doncaster during 1927 and 1928 went mainly to Stratford although Ardsley shed had use of a good many of them for a while after their delivery.

Things did not change too much over the years prior to WW2; Stratford shed had by far the largest number on its books with over a hundred in the early 1930's, with quite a few outstationed at sub sheds; Enfield Town, Ilford and Wood Street having reasonable numbers each. Smaller numbers could by found at varying times working from ex-GN sheds. Some of the Stratford engines were sub-shedded at Epping during WW2. Other ex-GER sheds such as Bury St Edmunds, Cambridge, Colchester, Ipswich, King's Lynn, Lowestoft, Norwich, Parkeston and Yarmouth all had N7's allocated at one time or another. Other ex GN sheds which used them included Boston, Bradford, Colwick, Copley Hill, Hornsey and Lincoln. Former GC sheds had a look-in too with Annesley, Staveley and Woodford all having a try. They even got onto the M&GN at Melton Constable in early BR days.

The engines fitted with push & pull gear in the BR period were sent to some interesting and diverse locations. The first five were allocated to Neasden in mid-1949 to work the Marylebone - South Ruislip interval service, an unsuccessful venture which lasted just a couple of years. Whilst on the former GC lines they also did some work on the Chesham branch. In 1951 these five engines all transferred to King's Cross shed to service the Finsbury Park-Alexandra Palace P&P trains. During that year three P&P fitted N7's were sent to Annesley to work the 'Dido'. These three went to the West Riding in 1954 along with one of the former King's Cross engines, to help work the diesel multiple unit services which had been thrown into disarray because of the numerous teething problems encountered with the d.m.u.'s. Auto-fitted N7's replaced other similarly fitted classes at Yarmouth, taking the place of F5's on the Lowestoft services to Beccles and Yarmouth. On the former London, Tilbury and Southend lines they replaced ex Midland 0-4-4 tanks at Plaistow and Tilbury sheds. Saffron Walden shed had some G5's which were equipped with push & pull apparatus and these were yet another class replaced by N7's. Cromer and King's Lynn sheds also had P&P N7's for a time in the mid and late 1950's.

With the expanding electrification in the London area and the introduction of more modern motive power, many N7's spent their latter days working from the country sheds of the former GER but more than half the class ended their days allocated to London area depots, the last batch working goods trains. Unlike most classes nearing the end of their working lives, some of the N7's were kept in highly polished condition by their crews at Wood Street and Enfield Town sheds whilst still employed on the Jazz services. No.69614 was specially painted in 1956 and achieved fame as West Side pilot at Liverpool Street station. The last examples of Class N7; 69621, 69632, 69640, 69646, 69671, 69692, 69697 and 69725, were all withdrawn together from Stratford depot on 9th September 1962.

Happily an N7 survives to this day - 69621 was purchased privately for preservation and is now resident at Chappel & Wakes Colne. It was the last locomotive built at Stratford.

Gorton again supplied another ten, Nos.2632 to 2641, built from 3rd November 1927 to 28th February 1928. They differed by having valve travel increased to $5^{23}/_{32}$in. which needed covers on the piano front plate under smokebox. The cab side window was further back and the bunker top was built up to eliminate coal rails. Two sunken footsteps were put into each side of the bunker and the cab rear windows were circular instead of square. A rear pony truck with 3ft 6in. wheels replaced the radial truck with 3ft 9in. wheels used hitherto.

Diagram 98:-

980 n409 8/25-8/31; 2656 11/31-1/34; 2636 6/34-9/36; 865 10/36-7/38; 2639 11/38-3/40; 913 8/40-1/43.

981 n421 9/25-7/31; 473 10/31-10/33; 460 5/34-11/35; 471 3/36-9/37; 2660 2/38-1/40; 947 5/40-11/42.

982 n426 10/25-5/32; 941 8/32-7/34; 2661 11/34-8/36; 2639 10/36-11/37; 988 4/38-1/40; 867 10/40-3/43; 2632 8/43-7/45.

983 n456 10/25-9/30; 457 12/30-3/32; 967 5/32-3/34; 832 8/34-5/36; 837 8/36-6/38; 828 8/38-7/40; 870 12/40-1/44.

984 n457 10/25-10/30; 2644 2/31-11/32; 865 2/33-1/35; 2648 8/35-8/37; 457 10/37-8/39; 971 12/39-4/42.

985 n460 11/25-3/34; 834 8/34-5/36; 988 7/36-3/38; 837 7/38-5/40; 826 9/40-2/43.

986 n464 11/25-11/32; 409 10/33-9/35; 457 1/36-9/37; 473 11/37-11/39; 918 1/40-5/42.

987 n471 11/25-3/32; 970 6/32-6/34; 2641 10/34-4/36; 916 7/36-10/37; 970 1/38-12/39; 834 3/40-10/42.

988 n473 11/25-8/31; 935 11/31-6/34; 987 10/34-7/36; 947 10/36-6/38; 464 8/38-6/40; 828 9/40-2/43.

989 n475 12/25-9/30; 913 1/31-3/33; 473 11/33-10/35; 966 1/36-10/37; 2639 12/37-10/38; 2653 2/39-12/40; 2635 5/41-11/43; 2642 2/44-2/46.

Diagram 30:-

990 n7990 12/23-5/30; 7995 8/30-6/32; 7992 10/32-9/34; 8011 5/35-11/36; 8002 1/37-8/38; 8003 11/38-6/40; 8002 7/40-3/44.

991 n7991 1/24-4/28; 8001 11/28-2/31; 8006 9/31-5/33; 7998 4/34-12/35; 8008 3/36-10/37; 7997 1/38-10/39; 8005 12/39-2/42.

992 n7992 1/24-8/30; 8000 9/31-5/33; 7996 11/33-7/35; 7995 11/35-6/37; 8007 9/37-5/39; 7998 8/39-6/40; 8010 12/40-8/43; 8009 10/43-11/45.

993 n7993 1/24-6/30; 8002 8/31-4/33; 8011 8/33-4/35; 7999 5/35-3/37; 7995 7/37-3/39; 8007 6/39-7/41.

994 n7994 1/24-7/32; 8005 5/33-12/34; 8000 2/35-10/36; 8010 2/37-9/40; 8000 11/40-5/43.

995 n7995 1/24-8/28; 7991 8/28-7/30; 7996 11/31-10/33; 8004 12/33-4/37; 7998 9/37-6/39; 8008 8/39-1/42.

996 n7996 1/24-3/28; 7995 7/28-1/30; 7991 10/30-6/34; 7990 9/34-6/36; 8005 9/36-4/38; 8001 5/38-12/39; 8006 3/40-2/42.

997 n7997 2/24-4/28; 7996 7/28-5/30; 7993 9/30-8/32; 8002 5/33-2/35; 8003 6/35-2/37; 7996 5/37-7/38; 8000 8/38-9/40; 8009 2/41-8/43.

998 n7998 2/24-4/30; 7999 9/30-9/32; 8000 6/33-1/35; 8002 3/35-11/36; 7999 5/37-11/38; 8009 1/39-1/41; 7990 9/41-12/43.

999 n7999 3/24-7/30; 8004 11/30-1/32; 7998 6/32-3/34; 8007 6/34-12/35; 7991 7/36-3/38; 8006 7/38-1/40; 7996 6/40-6/42; 8001 8/42-10/44.

1000 n8000 12/14-10/29.

1001 n8001 2/15-9/28; 7990 7/30-2/32; 7997 8/32-8/34; 7992 10/34-4/36.

1002 n8002 6/21-2/29; 8005 7/29-3/33; 8006 7/33-3/35; 7998 1/36-8/37; 7994 11/37-7/39; 7990 10/39-8/41.

1003 n8003 6/21-11/28; 8011 11/29-6/33; 8009 4/34-9/35; 8007 1/36-8/37; 7993 10/37-9/41.

1004 n8004 6/21-11/28; 8002 12/29-7/31; 8004 3/32-10/33; 7994 7/34-3/36; 7990 7/36-11/37; 7992 2/38-12/39.

1005 n8005 9/21-5/29; 8006 10/29-7/31; 7990 3/32-7/34; 8005 1/35-8/36; 8001 10/36-4/38.

1006 n8006 9/21-9/29; 8003 5/30-9/31; 8007 9/32-5/34; 7997 9/34-4/36; 8000 11/36-7/38; 8002 9/38-6/40; 7999 9/40-5/42.

1007 n8007 10/21-6/28; 8004 3/29-8/30; 8001 5/31-1/33; 8010 7/33-3/35; 8001 7/35-9/36; 8011 12/36-7/38; 7996 8/38-5/40.

1008 n8008 10/21-2/29; 8010 10/29-6/33; 8003 8/33-5/35; 7997 5/36-1/38; 7991 4/38-11/39; 8001 2/40-7/42.

1009 n8009 10/21-2/28; 8007 9/28-7/30; 7992 10/30-8/32; 8001 2/33-5/35; 8009 10/35-4/37; 8004 6/37-2/39; 7995 5/39-1/41.

1010 n8010 11/21-8/29; 7998 7/30-5/32; 7994 8/32-6/34; 8008 8/34-3/36; 7992 5/36-1/38; 8005 5/38-10/39; 7991 1/40-10/41.

1011 n8011 11/21-9/29; 8007 9/30-7/32; 8008 10/32-7/34; 8006 4/35-10/36.

Diagram 101:- Replacements built 1946-48.

1905 9663 7/46-3/49; 69733 7/49-3/56 r29048 10/51.

1906 9696 7/46-3/49; 69705 7/49-6/52.

1907 9650 8/46-8/49; 69713 10/49-6/52.

1908 9714 8/46-8/49; 69613 10/49-7/53 r29012 10/50.

1909 9726 8/46-12/48; 69704 3/49-11/51.

1910 9633 10/46-7/49; 69714 10/49-12/52.

1911 9608 9/46-3/48; 69609 8/48-11/50.

1912 9601 10/46-7/48; 69715 9/48-12/54 r29047 11/51.

1913 9677 11/46-5/49; 69729 8/49-6/52.

1914 9711 4/47-11/49; 69721 1/50-7/52.

1915 9707 11/47-5/50; 69719 7/50-3/52.

1916 9691 11/47-9/50.

1917 9649 12/47-8/50.

1918 9632 12/47-11/50.

1919 9706 1/48-5/48; 69721 3/49-5/51.

1920 9666 12/47-11/50.

1921 9656 1/48-9/50.

1922 9639 1/48-5/53 r29083 10/52.

1923 E9717 1/48-8/50.

1924 E9652 2/48-8/50.

1925 E9697 3/48-10/50.

1926 69686 6/48-9/50;

1927 69699 7/48-4/51.

1928 69601 10/48-1/51.

1929 69709 8/48-4/51.

Diagram 101:- Replacements built 1945.

1930 2651 4/45-10/47; 69604 3/48-9/50.

1931 7981 4/45-10/46; 9611 2/47-12/49; 69673 2/50-11/52.

1932 2605 4/45-9/47; 69605 8/48-12/50.

1933 2659 5/45-2/48; 69706 6/48-6/50.

1934 868 5/45-10/47; 69600 3/48-8/50.

1935 2601 6/45-10/49; 69685 12/49-3/52.

1936 409 5/45-7/47; 9708 10/47-5/50; 69717 9/50-4/53.

1937 2615 6/45-12/47; 69647 7/48-10/50.

1938 2607 6/45-6/48; 69692 9/48-3/51.

1939 826 6/45-10/47; E9610 2/48-7/50.

1940 2622 9/45-8/49; 69676 10/49-5/52.

1941 2613 9/45-8/48; 69725 10/48-6/51.

1942 907 10/45-1/48; 69612 9/48-2/51.

1943 7991 10/45-9/49; 69710 11/49-10/52.

1944 964 11/45-6/48; 69716 9/48-8/51.

1945 9725 2/46-8/48; 69678 12/48-12/50.

1946 873 12/45-8/48; 69728 10/48-11/51.

1947 9728 2/46-8/48; 69682 11/48-3/51.

1948 9702 2/46-10/51.

1949 9729 2/46-6/49; 69724 9/49-5/52.

Diagram 101:- Replacements built 1932-36.

1950 2604 5/32-6/34; 2602 8/34-5/36; 2614 8/36-4/38; 2620 3/39-12/40; 2616 4/41-2/44; 830 5/44-3/47; 9622 9/47-8/50.

1951 2605 6/32-6/36; 2615 3/37-10/38; 2616 5/39-3/41; 2625 8/41-2/44; 2628 5/44-10/46; 9636 5/47-9/50.

1952 2602 6/32-6/38; 2622 11/38-11/40; 2620 2/41-6/41; 7991 12/41-3/44; 7994 9/44-11/46; 9720 7/47-11/49; 69611 1/50-9/52 r29053 1/52.

1953 2606 6/36-1/38; 2601 10/38-6/39; 2611 8/40-9/42; 8010 10/43-10/45; 9721 3/46-2/49; 69731 6/49-7/52.

1954 2603 7/36-1/38; 2607 4/38-4/40; 2619 2/41-8/43; 2627 8/44-1/46; 9635 9/46-1/49; 69663 5/49-4/51.

1955 2605 7/36-4/38; 2619 2/39-12/40; 2629 5/41-2/44; 2652 8/44-3/46; 9727 6/46-12/48; 69635 3/49-2/52.

1956 2617 1/37-10/38; 2612 4/39-6/41; 2631 11/41-4/44; 2603 9/44-5/46; 9730 11/46-2/49; 69677 7/49-8/52 r29016 1/51.

Diagram 101:- Replacements built 1941-43.

1957 2610 6/41-12/43; 8005 3/44-5/46; 9704 8/46-2/49; 69687 9/49-12/51.

1958 2600 6/41-9/43; 8007 3/44-4/46; 9605 6/46-7/48; 69727 2/49-10/51.

1959 2624 6/41-1/44; 2612 4/44-9/44; 967 1/45-11/47; 69648 5/48-2/51.

1960 2613 8/41-8/43; 827 7/44-8/46; 9723 10/46-6/49; 69718 11/49-12/52 r29068 5/52.

1961 2612 7/41-3/44; 7991 5/44-9/45; 9617 2/46-10/48; 69603 5/49-7/51.

1962 8006 3/42-4/44; 2618 7/44-5/47; 9685 10/47-11/49; 69708 7/50-1/54 r29005 9/50.

1963 8005 4/42-1/44; 8006 6/44-6/46; 9603 12/46-3/49; 69667 9/49-5/52.

1964 7992 7/42-7/44; 9606 8/46-5/49; 69680 9/49-2/52.

1965 2605 2/43-3/45; 7990 11/45-7/48; 69617 11/48-9/51.

1966 2607 3/43-5/45; 2646 11/45-5/48; 69664 8/48-5/51.

1967 2615 8/43-5/45; 7982 9/45-2/48; 69615 5/48-3/52.

1968 2617 9/43-12/45; 9607 5/46-7/48; 69621 1/49-1/52.

1969 2622 9/43-7/45; 9621 2/46-7/47; 9701 10/47-5/50; 69649 9/50-5/53.

1970 2620 9/43-12/45; 9678 2/46-11/48; 69726 3/49-1/52.

1971 941 9/43-10/45; 9722 1/46-12/48; 69696 4/49-8/52 r29049 11/51.

1972 2613 10/43-8/45; 941 11/45-7/48; 69730 4/49-5/52.

1973 2619 10/43-2/46; 9705 6/46-6/49; 69616 9/49-6/52.

1974 2600 11/43-1/46; 9647 4/46-5/48; 69660 9/49-4/51.

1975 2626 12/43-1/46; 9692 4/46-8/48; 69675 7/49-11/52.

1976 2659 12/43-12/45; 9693 4/46-12/48; 69614 3/49-2/52.

1977 409 1/44-4/45; 9719 1/46-9/48; 69722 2/49-1/52.

1978 964 1/44-9/45; 9614 6/46-1/49; 69606 6/49-6/51.

1979 868 2/44-4/45; 9699 1/46-5/48; 69607 9/48-11/50.

1980 829 2/44-7/46; 9675 9/46-6/49; 69650 10/49-12/52.

1981 2629 3/44-7/46; 9713 3/47-10/49; 69711 12/49-3/53.

1982 2624 2/44-1/45; 2614 8/45-7/48; 69679 9/48-1/51.

1983 2602 3/44-6/46; 9718 2/47-10/49; 69732 12/49-8/52.

1984 2620 3/44-6/46; 9720 12/49-4/52.

1985 2625 3/44-5/46; 9731 8/46-5/49; 69723 8/49-8/52 r29035 6/51.

1986 7995 4/44-1/46; 9682 3/46-9/48; 69693 1/49-12/50.

Diagram 101:- Replacements built 1950.

1987 69684 5/50-2/55 r29038 8/51.

1988 69644 6/50-7/53.

1989 69707 6/50-3/53 r29066 4/52.

1990 69701 6/50-12/52.

1991 69630 7/50-5/54.

1992 69643 7/50-4/53.

1993 69640 8/50-11/53.

1994 69706 8/50-9/53.

Diagram 101 cont./
1995 69658 8/50-12/52.
1996 69610 8/50-1/53.

Diagram 98:-
2005 n826 1/26-5/32; 2638 8/32-9/34; 2660 12/34-6/36; 828 9/36-7/38; 941 11/38-9/40; 866 12/40-9/43.
2006 n827 2/26-3/32; 2641 8/32-9/34; 826 12/34-9/36; 2638 11/36-12/38; 2655 4/39-8/41; 2645 4/42-11/44; 2660 12/44-10/47; 9674 12/47-1/51.
2007 n828 2/26-8/32; 837 11/32-9/34; 2637 12/34-1/37; 460 9/37-5/39; 851 8/39-6/42; 919 9/42-1/45.
2008 n829 2/26-4/32; 2636 3/32-5/34; 828 10/34-8/36; 940 10/36-6/38; 2632 9/38-10/40; 952 1/41-12/43.
2009 n830 3/26-9/32; 852 12/32-11/34; 913 3/35-1/37; 2650 9/37-8/39; 970 1/40-5/42; 833 7/42-11/44.
2010 n832 3/26-6/32; 828 9/32-8/34; 940 11/34-9/36; 2644 11/36-12/38; 868 3/39-1/41; 2641 8/41-6/47.
2011 n833 4/26-5/30; 850 10/30-12/32; 475 10/33-8/35; 912 12/35-7/37; 968 9/37-7/39; 2650 10/39-1/43; 873 9/43-11/45; 9627 2/46-12/48; 69689 2/49-10/51.
2012 n834 4/26-8/32; 867 11/32-11/34; 865 3/35-9/36; 867 12/36-8/38; 2644 2/39-1/41; 460 9/41-1/46; 9688 3/46-8/48.
2013 n837 6/26-10/32; 2655 12/32-9/34; 2647 1/35-?/36; 907 1/37-10/38; 2646 3/39-3/41; 471 10/41-11/43; 475 1/44-3/46.
2014 n838 6/26-8/32; 830 10/32-10/34; 852 1/35-1/37; 2649 3/37-7/39; 456 11/39-2/42; 457 4/42-8/44.
2015 n850 7/26-7/30; 940 10/30-10/32; 850 2/33-1/35; 853 7/35-7/37; 2654 9/37-11/39; 838 2/40-3/42; 950 5/42-12/44.
2016 n851 7/26-1/32; 971 3/32-4/34; 988 8/34-6/36; 941 9/36-10/38; 866 2/39-11/40; 2646 4/41-10/43.
2017 n852 8/26-11/32; 2642 1/33-11/34; 2649 3/35-2/37; 868 4/37-1/39; 2635 6/39-4/41; 2648 3/42-3/44; 912 6/44-9/46; 9680 2/47-8/49.
2018 n853 9/26-5/33; 2656 3/34-3/36; 2632 7/36-8/38; 873 11/38-10/40; 2644 3/41-9/43.
2019 n865 10/26-1/33; 2648 11/33-6/35; 829 10/35-6/37; 2645 1/38-11/39; 833 2/40-6/42; 947 1/43-4/45; 2633 5/45-10/47; 9695 1/48-1/51.
2020 n866 10/26-5/31; 421 9/31-9/33; 964 3/34-11/35; 833 6/36-2/38; 832 5/38-2/40; 919 8/40-8/42; 2634 3/43-4/45; 834 5/45-11/47; E9684 2/48-3/50.
2021 n867 11/26-10/32; 2648 12/32-10/33; 967 4/34-1/36; 2641 6/36-11/37; 950 1/38-11/39; 988 2/40-3/42; 2661 7/42-8/47; 9671 10/47-11/49.
2022 n868 12/26-5/31; 2651 9/31-10/33; 971 5/34-1/36; 970 5/36-12/37; 830 1/38-9/39; 2645 12/39-2/42; 970 7/42-12/47; E9640 3/48-6/50.
2023 n870 12/26-4/31; 866 7/31-4/33; 2651 11/33-5/35; 2658 4/36-10/37; 834 3/38-2/40; 464 7/40-8/42; 2654 12/42-10/45; 9629 1/46-10/48.
2024 n873 2/27-10/32; 2644 12/32-11/34; 2643 4/35-3/37; 475 6/37-1/39; 912 5/39-5/41; 456 3/42-7/47.
2025 n907 10/25-8/30; 475 11/30-1/32; 2640 4/32-6/34; 2639 10/34-9/36; 464 11/36-7/38; 2647 11/38-?/40; 475 4/41-12/43.
2026 n912 10/25-12/31; 475 2/32-9/33; 918 4/34-2/36; 2633 5/36-6/38; 865 8/38-9/40; 907 11/40-5/43.
2027 n913 10/25-11/30; 2643 6/31-5/33; 966 3/34-12/35; 971 2/36-12/37; 833 3/38-1/40; 935 5/40-11/42; 940 6/43-6/45; 2632 8/45-8/47; 9637 11/47-12/49.
2028 n916 10/25-7/32; 834 10/32-7/34; 830 11/34-3/36; 2634 7/36-6/38; 2637 1/39-5/41; 426 12/41-6/44.
2029 n918 10/25-3/32; 826 7/32-10/34; 873 2/35-2/36; 834 6/36-2/38; 2636 7/38-8/40; 2653 1/41-9/43.
2030 n919 10/25-9/32; 873 11/32-1/35; 2650 7/35-8/37; 2640 10/37-6/39; 966 10/39-12/41; 2658 5/42-5/45; 828 7/45-2/48; 69646 9/48-7/51.
2031 n935 11/25-9/31; 851 2/32-5/35; 475 9/35-5/37; 421 7/37-4/39; 968 8/39-2/42; 916 7/42-10/46; 9667 1/47-7/49.
2032 n940 11/25-8/30; 456 10/30-1/33; 2643 6/33-2/35; 2654 8/35-8/37; 971 1/38-10/39; 2633 5/40-10/42; 913 3/43-5/45; 2658 6/45-3/48; 69688 10/48-3/51.
2033 n941 11/25-7/32; 838 9/32-8/34; 2655 11/34-3/36; 2648 9/37-9/39; 916 1/40-5/42; 2633 11/42-4/45; 837 6/45-12/47; 69634 5/48-12/50.
2034 n947 11/25-9/32; 2654 6/33-7/35; 968 11/35-8/37; 827 10/37-8/39; 2654 12/39-11/42; 2650 4/43-5/46.
2035 n950 11/25-9/32; 866 7/33-6/35; 832 7/36-4/38; 2661 8/38-5/40; 2640 1/41-4/42; 834 11/42-4/45; 913 6/45-12/47; 69661 5/48-12/50.
2036 n952 12/25-4/32; 832 7/32-6/34; 838 10/34-7/36; 2657 10/36-7/38; 913 10/38-7/40; 2647 12/40-?/44; 853 1/45-8/47; 9700 11/47-12/50.
2037 n964 12/25-3/32; 426 6/32-9/34; 919 2/35-10/36; 952 12/36-12/38; 2659 2/39-7/40; 409 3/41-11/43; 2635 1/44-8/46.
2038 n965 12/25-2/32; 952 5/32-8/34; 907 11/34-12/36; 873 2/37-10/38; 2643 3/39-2/42; 464 9/42-9/47; 9673 12/47-1/50.
2039 n967 12/25-4/32; 2635 8/32-11/34; 850 2/35-3/37; 851 5/37-7/39; 2648 11/39-2/42; 971 6/42-8/47; 9672 10/47-8/50.
2040 n968 12/25-1/32; 457 4/32-6/34; 941 10/34-8/36; 2655 1/37-3/39; 460 6/39-8/41; 2651 3/42-2/45.
2041 n970 12/25-4/32; 916 9/32-7/34; 2638 10/34-10/36; 913 2/37-9/38; 2642 12/38-1/41; 2637 7/41-3/44.
2042 n971 1/26-1/32; 918 4/32-4/34; 916 8/34-6/36; 838 8/36-5/38; 940 7/38-6/40; 2656 10/40-7/43.
2043 n987 1/26-5/32; 2637 9/32-11/34; 2646 2/35-3/37; 2643 5/37-2/39; 852 5/39-12/41; 851 7/42-11/44; 852 1/45-11/47; E9668 2/48-9/50.

2044 n988 1/26-9/32; 940 11/32-10/34; 2635 1/35-3/37; 471 10/37-5/39; 827 9/39-9/41; 2643 4/42-5/45; 865 7/45-7/48.
2045 n2632 11/27-11/31; 829 2/32-1/34; 471 6/34-2/36; 2656 4/36-4/38; 2657 8/38-4/40; 865 10/40-4/43; 2653 10/43-3/46; 9623 5/46-11/48; 69631 5/49-6/52.
2046 n2633 11/27-1/32; 966 4/32-1/34; 457 7/34-1/36; 873 2/36-1/37; 866 3/37-12/38; 475 3/39-2/41; 2655 9/41-12/47; 69657 3/48-11/50.
2047 n2634 11/27-3/32; 987 7/32-8/34; 837 11/34-7/36; 2653 1/37-1/39; 471 6/39 9/41; 964 12/41-11/43; 421 2/44-4/46.
2048 n2635 11/27-7/32; 919 10/32-12/34; 870 7/35-12/36; 852 2/37-3/39; 853 9/39-7/42; 935 1/43-5/45; 2643 6/45-10/47; 9644 1/48-5/50.
2049 n2636 12/27-1/32; 964 4/32-2/34; 2640 7/34-4/36; 935 6/36-2/38; 426 5/38-2/40; 2657 6/40-10/42; 828 4/43-5/45; 940 8/45-1/48; 69694 6/48-10/50.
2050 n2637 12/27-7/32; 2639 10/32-8/34; 426 11/34-7/36; 2636 10/36-6/38; 826 9/38-7/40; 2632 12/40-5/43; 2637 5/44-8/46; 9655 12/46-6/49.
2051 n2638 1/28-7/32; 988 10/32-7/34; 2657 11/34-9/36; 919 10/36-7/38; 870 1/39-11/40; 829 6/41-12/43; 870 3/44-6/46; 9644 9/46-9/49.
2052 n2639 1/28-9/32; 2647 12/32-?/34; 851 6/35-4/37; 853 8/37-8/39; 950 12/39-4/42; 987 10/42-11/47; E9654 2/48-3/51.
2053 n2640 2/28-2/32; 2634 4/32-7/34; 952 10/34-10/36; 964 9/37-6/39; 2641 9/39-7/41; 966 1/42-11/46; 9630 4/47-650.
2054 n2641 2/28-6/32; 947 11/32-7/34; 2634 9/34-6/36; 2661 9/36-6/38; 952 1/39-12/40; 912 6/41-5/44; 457 9/44-11/46; 9638 6/47-12/49; 69637 1/50-11/52.

Diagram 101:-
2055 n2600 11/27-2/33; 2625 5/33-5/35; 2600 6/35-4/37; 2629 7/37-5/39; 2630 9/39-11/41; 7997 2/42-7/44; 7979 11/44-8/46; 9619 11/46-3/49; 69602 6/49-9/51 r29006 9/50.
2056 n2601 11/27-6/32; 2602 8/32-7/34; 2606 10/34-5/36; 2601 12/36-9/38; 2615 12/38-9/40; 2622 12/40-7/43.
2057 n2602 11/27-7/32; 2603 8/32-3/34; 2604 7/34-5/36; 2626 3/37-10/38; 2600 5/39-5/41; 2618 11/41-6/44; 2632 9/44-9/47.
2058 n2603 11/27-7/32; 2614 9/32-5/34; 2607 10/34-9/36; 2625 6/37-4/39; 2606 1/40-5/42; 2611 10/42-1/45; 2604 2/45-11/47.
2059 n2604 11/27-4/32; 2609 7/32-2/34; 2603 6/34-5/36; 2622 3/37-10/38; 2613 4/39-5/41; 2627 12/41-6/44; 7997 8/44-10/46; 9616 1/47-7/49.
2060 n2605 11/27-4/32; 2601 7/32-12/34; 2613 2/35-2/37; 2620 5/37-2/39; 2624 5/39-5/41; 2609 2/42-2/47; 9687 5/47-8/49; 69703 11/49-8/52.
2061 n2606 12/27-1/33; 2623 3/33-4/35; 2621 7/35-7/37; 2604 2/38-2/40; 8011 4/40-8/42; 8003 11/42-2/45.
2062 n2607 12/27-10/32; 2615 1/33-1/35; 2620 5/35-3/37; 2616 5/37-4/39; 2602 8/39-1/42; 2603 5/42-8/44; 2612 10/44-6/46.
2063 n2608 12/27-2/34; 2614 7/34-7/36; 2610 4/37-2/39; 2629 6/39-3/41; 2630 1/42-7/44; 2606 11/44-8/47; 9732 11/47-11/49; 69638 1/50-3/53.
2064 n2609 12/27-6/32; 2611 10/32-12/36; 2621 9/37-10/39; 7992 2/40-5/42; 8011 10/42-11/44.
2065 n2610 1/28-1/33; 2600 3/33-5/35; 2630 7/35-6/37; 2606 2/38-12/39; 2604 3/40-6/42; 8004 9/43-7/45; 7978 10/45-6/47; 9698 7/48-2/51.
2066 n2611 1/28-8/32; 2619 11/32-9/34; 2617 12/34-11/36; 2618 6/37-5/39; 2631 8/39-10/41; 7994 2/42-8/44; 7989 12/44-12/46; 9620 8/47-8/50.
2067 n2612 1/28-10/32; 2607 12/32-8/34; 2619 11/34-12/36; 2611 1/37-9/38; 2610 3/39-4/41; 2620 8/41-7/43; 2623 11/43-1/46.
2068 n2613 1/28-10/32; 2621 12/32-6/35; 2629 7/35-6/37; 2603 2/38-1/40; 2605 6/40-12/42; 867 5/43-6/45.
2069 n2614 2/28-7/32; 2616 10/32-1/35; 2615 4/35-1/37; 2628 7/37-5/39; 2627 9/39-11/41; 2602 2/42-1/44; 2616 3/44-12/46.
2070 n2616 2/28-9/32; 2613 11/32-12/34; 2616 3/35-4/37; 2630 7/37-8/39; 2614 6/40-12/42; 2601 6/43-5/45; 7993 6/45-3/48; 9651 9/48-9/51.
2071 n2615 2/28-12/32; 2622 2/33-1/35; 2618 5/35-5/37; 2623 7/37-3/39; 2601 8/39-10/40; 2626 1/41-10/43; 2610 1/44-5/46.
2072 n2617 3/28-9/34; 2601 1/35-11/36; 2619 1/37-1/39; 2623 5/39-4/41; 2628 8/41-4/44; 2621 9/44-9/46; 9733 1/47-6/49; 69633 8/49-9/51.
2073 n2618 4/28-1/33; 2606 2/33-9/34; 2626 1/35-1/37; 2613 4/37-3/39; 2625 6/39-6/41; 2608 1/42-2/44; 2631 6/44-12/46.
2074 n2619 6/28-10/32; 2612 11/32-1/35; 2610 3/35-3/37; 2609 12/37-9/39; 2601 12/40-4/43; 2639 12/43-2/46; 9712 6/46-12/48; 69619 4/49-5/52.
2075 n2621 7/28-11/32; 2624 2/33-4/35; 2627 6/35-6/37; 2614 5/38-5/40; 2623 5/41-9/43; 2639 1/44-1/46.
2076 n2620 6/28-3/33; 2628 5/33-4/35; 2625 7/35-5/37; 2627 7/37-8/39; 2609 11/39-1/42; 2604 9/42-1/45; 2624 3/45-6/46; 9676 9/46-9/49; 69625 2/50-9/55 r29080 10/52.
2077 n2624 9/28-12/32; 2618 2/33-3/35; 2628 7/35-6/37; 2608 9/37-5/39; 2621 12/39-12/41; 2606 6/42-10/44; 2611 2/45-2/47; 9669 9/47-3/53 r29044 9/51.
2078 n2622 7/28-1/33; 2610 2/33-1/35; 2622 4/35-1/37; 2612 4/37-3/39; 2608 7/39-12/41; 8008 8/43-8/44; 2647 12/44-3/47; 9621 8/47-11/48; 69712 2/49-11/51.
2079 n2623 7/28-2/33; 2620 4/33-3/35; 2624 6/35-3/37; 2600 5/37-3/39; 2628 6/39-6/41; 8007 9/41-2/44.
2080 n2625 9/28-3/33; 2626 7/33-11/34; 2612 3/35-3/37; 2624 5/37-3/39; 2618 7/39-10/41; 2621 1/42-7/44; 7986 9/44-7/46.
2081 n2626 10/28-6/33; 2627 9/33-4/35; 2623 7/35-6/37; 2631 8/37-7/39; 2603 2/40-4/42; 2614 3/43-6/45.
2082 n2627 10/28-8/33; 2608 3/34-10/35; 2609 3/36-11/37; 2611 10/38-6/40; 2615 10/40-6/43; 2646 12/43-10/45; 9679 2/46-8/48; 69719 11/48-5/50.
2083 n2628 11/28-3/33; 2630 6/33-5/35; 2631 11/35-7/37; 2602 3/38-6/39; 2607 5/40-12/42; 826 5/43-6/45; 867 7/45-4/48.

Diagram 101 cont./
2084 n2629 11/28-8/33; 2631 10/33-10/35; 2604 6/36-1/38; 2626 12/38-11/40;
  2617 1/41-6/43; 866 11/43-2/46.
2085 n2630 12/28-5/33; 2629 9/33-6/35; 2608 11/35-7/37; 2605 5/38-4/40; 8003 7/40-9/42;
  8000 7/43-9/45; 7988 11/45-1/48; 69608 7/48-12/50.
2086 n2631 12/28-9/33; 2609 3/34-2/36; 2607 10/36-3/38; 2617 12/38-12/40;
  8004 3/41-7/43; 7990 1/44-10/45.

Diagram 98:-
2087 n2642 6/27-11/30; 868 7/31-10/33; 968 1/34-10/35; 460 12/35-8/37; 456 1/38-6/38;
  867 10/38-8/40; 941 12/40-7/43; 2648 4/44-2/46; 9631 5/46-3/49; 69626 7/49-8/51.
2088 n2643 7/27-4/31; 2654 7/31-5/33; 2650 8/33-6/35; 421 10/35-5/37; 2658 11/37-10/39;
  2660 2/40-10/44; 2640 3/45-1/47; 9681 8/47-8/49; 69624 10/49-11/52 r27850 9/50.
2089 n2644 7/27-12/30; 870 6/31-6/33; 2659 9/33-6/35; 830 4/36-12/37; 456 7/38-10/39;
  473 12/39-4/42; 853 8/42-12/44; 850 2/45-3/48; 69623 12/48-5/52 r27852 1/51.
2090 n2645 7/27-9/33; 2633 4/34-4/36; 426 8/36-4/38; 2633 7/38-4/40; 2634 8/40-1/43;
  907 8/43-9/45; 2649 12/45-1/49; 69690 5/49-6/51.
2091 n2646 7/27-11/32; 456 2/33-7/36; 2642 10/36-11/38; 2638 1/39-2/41; 421 8/41-1/44.
2092 n2647 7/27-?/32; 2652 1/33-12/34; 866 7/35-2/37; 2635 4/37-4/39; 967 10/39-2/42;
  473 5/42-8/44; 988 11/44-8/47; 9628 11/47-7/51.
2093 n2648 7/27-11/32; 907 1/33-10/34; 2652 2/35-2/37; 2646 4/37-2/39; 964 7/39-11/41;
  838 5/42-10/44; 918 11/44-11/47.
2094 n2649 8/27-6/31; 2655 8/31-11/32; 2646 1/33-1/35; 868 7/35-3/37; 850 4/37-5/39;
  2651 8/39-2/42; 988 4/42-10/44; 833 1/45-5/47; 9625 9/47-11/49.
2095 n2650 8/27-7/33; 421 10/33-8/35; 964 1/36-7/37; 2641 12/37-8/39; 987 5/40-9/42;
  837 2/43-5/45; 935 6/45-12/47; 69698 5/48-8/50.
2096 n2651 8/27-7/31; 409 10/31-9/33; 912 3/34-11/35; 918 3/36-1/38; 935 3/38-4/40;
  837 6/40-12/42; 865 6/43-6/45; 2644 9/45-12/47; 69659 3/48-10/50.
2097 n2652 8/27-11/32; 853 6/33-7/35; 473 11/35-10/37; 918 2/38-12/39; 426 3/40-11/41;
  968 5/42-3/45; 947 5/45-3/48; 69627 1/49-6/51.
2098 n2653 8/27-9/31; 2661 12/31-9/34; 2653 11/34-12/36; 2652 3/37-4/39;
  2640 8/39-10/40; 2652 5/41-6/44; 832 11/44-9/47; 9670 12/47-9/50.
2099 n2654 8/27-5/31; 2649 8/31-1/33; 870 7/33-5/35; 967 2/36-9/37; 966 11/37-9/39;
  2658 12/39-3/42; 832 5/42-10/44; 2645 12/44-8/47; 9645 11/47-10/52.
2100 n2655 8/27-6/31; 2658 10/31-4/34; 947 9/34-8/36; 826 10/36-8/38; 907 11/38-9/40;
  868 3/41-1/44.
2101 n2656 8/27-9/31; 2632 1/32-6/36; 2659 2/37-1/39; 829 5/39-5/41; 852 1/42-12/44;
  950 1/45-5/47.
2102 n2657 8/27-9/34; 867 1/35-10/36; 2651 6/37-7/39; 830 10/39-8/41; 850 5/42-12/44;
  919 2/45-1/48; 69642 6/48-2/51.
2103 n2658 9/27-7/31; 2653 11/31-10/34; 2644 1/35-10/36; 409 7/37-1/39; 2652 6/39-4/41;
  830 10/41-4/44.
2104 n2660 9/27-1/32; 471 5/32-5/34; 970 7/34-4/36; 987 8/36-5/38; 919 8/38-6/40;
  2636 10/40-3/44.
2105 n2659 9/27-8/33; 2645 10/33-11/35; 827 2/36-10/37; 916 12/37-11/39; 2661 7/40-6/42;
  2657 12/42-3/45; 2634 5/45-11/47; E9658 1/48-7/50.
2106 n2661 9/27-10/31; 912 2/32-2/34; 2658 5/34-3/36; 456 7/36-12/37; 987 6/38-3/40;
  940 7/40-4/43; 2644 10/43-9/45; 2654 11/45-5/48; 69629 11/48-9/52.

Diagram 30:- Replacements for N7/GE.
2107 8009 6/28-5/32; 7995 8/32-3/34; 7991 8/34-6/36; 8006 12/36-6/38; 8011 8/38-3/40;
  7998 7/40-1/42; 7999 5/42-1/46; 9618 6/46-5/48.
2108 7997 7/28-7/32; 7993 9/32-8/34; 8010 4/35-12/36; 8003 3/37-10/38; 7999 12/38-7/40;
  7995 3/41-3/44; 8002 5/44-9/46.
2109 8002 5/29-5/31; 8003 10/31-7/33; 7995 5/34-10/35; 7993 3/36-9/37; 8008 11/37-6/39;
  7994 9/39-12/41; 7996 7/42-5/46; 9602 10/46-6/49.
2110 8003 2/29-3/30; 7996 7/30-9/31; 8007 9/32-3/34; 7993 9/34-2/36; 7994 4/36-10/37;
  7990 12/37-9/39; 7997 11/39-1/42; 7998 3/42-6/47.
2111 8008 5/29-8/32; 7999 10/32-4/35; 7996 8/35-3/37; 8009 5/37-12/38; 8004 3/39-2/41;
  7993 10/41-5/45; 7987 12/45-6/48.

Diagram 98:- Replacements for N7/1 & N7/2.
2112 2633 2/32-3/34; 827 6/34-1/36; 950 3/36-12/37; 2634 7/38-6/40; 873 12/40-7/43;
  2656 11/43-5/46; 9665 12/46-6/49; 69653 9/49-7/52.
2113 968 2/32-12/33; 829 3/34-10/35; 2645 12/35-11/37; 2656 6/38-8/40; 2642 3/41-12/43;
  2636 4/44-7/46; 9662 6/47-8/52.
2114 833 6/30-7/32; 950 10/32-2/36; 2640 5/36-9/37; 838 6/38-1/40; 2639 4/40-11/43;
  426 7/44-8/46; 9653 11/46-7/49; 69681 9/49-3/52.
2115 2660 3/32-11/34; 2642 1/35-9/36; 2637 2/37-12/38; 421 6/39-7/41; 827 10/41-5/44;
  473 10/44-3/47; 9643 8/47-6/50.
2116 833 9/32-5/36; 870 1/37-12/38; 850 6/39-3/42; 2640 5/42-2/45; 968 4/45-12/46;
  9641 7/47-8/52.
2117 2642 1/31-12/32; 2649 3/33-1/35; 2651 6/35-5/37; 829 7/37-3/39; 457 9/39-2/42;
  967 4/42-12/44; 851 1/45-6/47.
2118 464 1/33-10/36; 2647 12/36-?/38; 409 3/39-1/41; 2638 4/41-11/43; 952 1/44-5/46;
  9626 1/47-5/49; 69685 8/49-5/52.
2119 827 4/32-5/34; 935 7/34-4/36; 2660 7/36-1/38; 947 7/38-4/40; 2659 8/40-10/43;
  471 12/43-12/45; 9690 6/46-4/49; 9655 8/49-1/53.
2120 868 10/33-7/35; 409 9/35-5/37; 912 8/37-4/39; 2649 9/39-4/42; 918 6/42-10/44;
  838 11/44-6/47; 9683 12/47-10/52.
2121 907 10/30-12/32; 913 4/33-2/35; 2659 7/35-1/37; 967 10/37-8/39; 832 4/40-4/42;
  2649 6/42-11/45.

Diagram 101:- Replacements built 1955-57.
24800 69663 12/55-3/58; 69712 5/58-12/60w.
24801 69672 8/56-10/59w; 69640 2/60-9/62w.
24802 69648 9/56-8/60w.
24803 69651 3/57-1/61w.
24804 69633 12/57-8/59w; 69733 10/59-10/60w.

Diagram 98:- Renumbered boilers.
27850 69624 r2088 -11/52.
27851 69694 12/50-10/54.
27852 69623 r2089 -5/52.
27853 69695 2/51-12/54.
27854 69627 8/51-1/54.
27855 69690 9/51-11/54; 69695 1/55-12/58w.
27856 69646 8/51-4/54.
27857 69689 12/51-3/57w.
27858 69626 9/51-2/54.
27859 69631 8/52-2/55.
27860 69662 9/52-1/55.
27861 69629 10/52-3/56.
27862 69683 11/52-11/54.
27863 69645 11/52-4/55.
27864 69637 12/52-8/55.
27865 69624 1/53-10/55.
27866 69627 2/54-8/56.

Diagram 101:- Renumbered boilers.
29000 69620 9/50-2/55; 69670 10/55-11/57; 69631 1/58-1/61w.
29001 69622 9/50-2/53; 69693 5/53-8/55; 69658 11/55-2/58; 69720 8/58-11/60w.
29002 69656 10/50-7/53; 69618 10/53-4/57.
29003 69600 9/50-1/53; 69700 4/53-5/56; 69660 11/56-5/59w; 69732 8/59-9/61w.
29004 69652 9/50-10/53; 69678 1/54-5/56; 69664 10/56-11/60w.
29005 69708 r1962 -1/54; 69642 1/55-6/58; 69677 10/58-11/60w.
29006 69602 r2055 -9/51; 69727 11/51-3/55.
29007 69604 11/50-12/52; 69659 3/53-1/56; 69602 9/56-7/59w; 69675 9/59-6/61w.
29008 69686 10/50-2/53.
29009 69691 10/50-8/53; 69603 11/53-10/56; 69646 12/56-7/59.
29010 69659 11/50-2/53; 69672 5/53-6/56; 69634 11/56-1/59w.
29011 69697 11/50-6/53; 69636 12/53-1/57; 69606 3/57-8/58w.
29012 69613 r1908 -7/53; 69633 10/53-7/55; 69676 1/56-2/59w.
29013 69647 11/50-6/54; 69702 9/54-3/58.
29014 69657 1/51-9/53; 69640 12/53-5/56; 69698 12/56-9/59; 69724 12/59-9/61w.
29015 69609 12/50-1/53; 69638 5/53-3/56; 69706 1/57-12/60w.
29016 69677 r1956 -8/52; 69723 10/52-12/55; 69628 5/56-12/58w.
29017 69605 1/51-1/53; 69670 4/53-8/55; 69643 3/56-5/58w; 69701 10/58-12/60w.
29018 69634 2/51-5/53; 69666 7/53-7/56; 69699 12/56-11/60w.
29019 69608 1/51-5/53; 69691 8/53-8/56; 69679 5/57-1/61w.
29020 69601 2/51-3/53; 69639 7/53-2/56; 69666 9/56-3/59w; 69700 6/59-12/60w.
29021 69679 2/51-2/54; 69620 3/55-8/57; 69604 11/57-8/59w; 69653 10/59-5/62w.
29022 69642 3/51-11/54; 69726 6/55-8/58; 69727 10/58-11/60w.
29023 69618 3/51-9/53; 69694 11/54-11/60w.
29024 69643 3/51-8/53; 69657 10/53-2/57; 69692 4/58-9/62w.
29025 69692 4/51-6/55; 69623 11/55-2/59w.
29026 69654 4/51-7/55; 69733 4/56-8/59; 69714 10/59-9/61w.
29027 69688 4/51-7/53; 69617 10/54-7/57; 69611 11/57-11/60w.
29028 69660 5/51-1/54; 69667 11/54-3/57; 69665 8/57-2/60w.
29029 69699 5/51-10/53; 69671 12/54-3/57; 69662 8/57-5/59w; 69698 11/59-9/61w.
29030 69663 5/51-5/53; 69656 8/53-9/57.
29031 69709 6/51-2/54; 69664 6/54-9/56; 69683 5/57-2/60w.
29032 69664 6/51-5/54; 69719 4/55-5/59; 69687 8/59-12/60w.
29033 69721 7/51-1/54; 69685 4/54-1/57; 69647 1/58-11/60w.
29034 69725 8/51-6/54; 69722 4/55-5/58; 69642 8/58-11/60w.
29035 69723 r1985 -8/52; 69703 10/52-8/55; 69607 12/55-7/58w.
29036 69606 8/51-9/53; 69699 11/53-11/56; 69657 3/57-6/59w.
29037 69603 8/51-10/53; 69721 2/54-1/58; 69693 9/58-9/61w.
29038 69684 r1987 -2/55; 69645 5/55-9/57; 69709 3/58-11/60w.
29039 69628 8/51-4/56; 69697 6/56-10/59.
29040 69716 9/51-1/55; 69720 4/55-6/58.
29041 69651 10/51-7/54; 69715 1/55-5/58; 69704 9/58-10/60w.
29042 69617 10/51-9/54; 69681 11/54-2/57; 69684 8/57-8/60w.
29043 69712 12/51-1/55.
29044 69669 r2077 -3/53; 69682 8/53-11/55.
29045 69602 11/51-1/54; 69709 3/54-2/58; 69654 6/58-12/60w.
29046 69633 10/51-9/53; 69612 7/54-8/59w; 69725 10/59-9/62w.
29047 69715 r1912 -12/54; 69665 3/55-7/57.
29048 69733 r1905 -3/56; 69627 9/56-3/59w; 69730 8/59-9/61w.
29049 69696 r1971 -8/52; 69645 12/52-4/56; 69700 6/56-5/59.
29050 69702 11/51-8/54; 69728 7/55-4/59.
29051 69728 12/51-5/55; 69668 10/55-11/57; 69690 1/58-1/61w.
29052 69704 1/52-3/55; 69703 9/55-1/59w.
29053 69611 r1952 -9/52; 69673 12/52-10/55; 69688 5/56-10/58; 69719 6/59-11/60w.
29054 69687 1/52-5/54; 69725 8/54-1/57; 69667 5/57-2/59w.

29055 69722 2/52-3/55; 69615 5/55-9/60w.
29056 69621 2/52-1/56; 69626 10/56-6/59w; 69707 10/59-4/61w.
29057 69635 3/52-9/55; 69624 12/55-12/58w.
29058 69726 2/52-5/55; 69731 7/55-2/59w.
29059 69680 3/52-7/54; 69604 6/55-9/57; 69668 12/57-9/61w.
29060 69614 4/52-9/55; 69724 12/55-10/59.
29061 69615 4/52-4/55; 69610 12/55-1/59w.
29062 69719 4/52-3/55; 69625 10/55-4/59w.
29063 69681 4/52-10/54; 69729 8/55-4/59; 69723 7/59-9/61w.
29064 69685 5/52-3/54; 69687 6/54-1/57.
29065 69720 5/52-3/55; 69692 8/55-3/58; 69722 6/58-12/60w.
29066 69707 r1989 -3/53; 69717 5/53-10/56.
29067 69724 6/52-10/55; 69730 7/56-6/59; 69678 9/59-9/61w.
29068 69718 r1960 -12/52; 69610 2/53-11/55; 69659 2/56-1/59w.
29069 69619 6/52-6/55; 69605 1/56-10/58w.
29070 69676 6/52-12/55; 69650 3/56-5/59w.
29071 69623 6/52-9/55; 69621 3/56-12/59.
29072 69665 7/52-1/55.
29073 69616 7/52-6/55; 69637 10/55-3/59w.
29074 69705 8/52-8/56; 69718 2/57-12/60w.
29075 69653 9/52-6/56; 69655 11/56-8/59w.
29076 69731 9/52-6/55; 69669 8/55-10/57.
29077 69607 9/52-10/55; 69613 11/55-11/59w; 69632 8/60-9/62w.
29078 69641 9/52-8/55; 69714 12/55-9/59; 69697 11/59-9/62w.
29079 69732 10/52-1/56; 69639 3/56-1/59w.
29080 69625 r2076 -9/55; 69673 11/55-9/58.
29081 69696 9/52-4/55; 69600 9/55-2/58; 69663 5/58-11/60w.
29082 69611 10/52-6/55; 69635 10/55-3/59w.
29083 69639 r1922 -5/53; 69688 9/53-4/56; 69608 8/56-8/58w.
29084 69710 11/52-6/56; 69653 9/56-9/59; 69671 12/59-9/62w.
29085 69650 1/53-1/56; 69710 7/56-9/61w.
29086 69718 1/53-1/57; 69671 4/57-10/59; 69621 3/60-9/62w.
29087 69701 2/53-11/55; 69707 5/55-9/59; 69646 10/59-9/62w.
29088 69600 2/53-8/55; 69713 10/55-4/59.
29089 69604 1/53-5/55; 69701 1/56-9/58; 69728 5/59-9/61w.
29090 69655 2/53-10/56; 69645 10/57-11/60w.
29091 69622 3/53-5/56; 69661 8/56-10/59w.
29092 69668 8/53-7/55; 69693 10/55-8/58; 69696 4/59-4/61w.
29093 69608 6/53-6/56; 69705 9/56-6/59w.
29094 69661 9/53-5/56; 69691 9/56-12/60w.

Diagram 101:- Replacements built 1955.
29095 69712 3/55-4/58; 69715 6/58-12/60w.
29096 69631 3/55-12/57; 69658 3/58-4/61w.
29097 69684 4/55-6/57; 69656 11/57-4/61w.
29098 69704 4/55-8/58; 69688 11/58-11/60w.
29099 69727 4/55-9/58; 69729 5/59-12/60w.

Diagram 101:- Replacements ordered in 1950 and originally numbered 1890 - 1904.
29100 69698 9/50-6/54; 69651 8/54-2/57; 69708 5/57-1/61w.
29101 69672 9/50-4/53; 69663 6/53-11/55; 69644 1/56-1/59w.

29102 69668 10/50-3/53; 69607 5/53-10/55; 69609 12/55-4/58w.
29103 69636 10/50-11/53; 69660 1/54-10/56; 69711 12/56-11/59w.
29104 69670 11/50-3/53; 69643 5/53-2/56; 69638 5/56-5/59w.
29105 69666 12/50-6/53; 69697 7/53-4/56; 69678 7/56-7/59.
29106 69607 1/51-4/53; 69649 6/53 2/56; 69675 6/56-8/59.
29107 69632 12/50-8/53; 69706 10/53-12/56; 69681 3/57-12/60w.
29108 69700 1/51-2/53; 69601 4/53-1/56; 69686 3/56-8/58; 69713 5/59-9/61w.
29109 69661 1/51-7/53; 69648 9/53-8/56; 69652 11/56-12/60w.
29110 69693 1/51-3/53; 69634 6/53-10/56; 69725 2/57 8/59.
29111 69678 1/51-12/53; 69679 3/54-3/57; 69669 11/57-4/59w.
29112 69674 2/51-11/53; 69620 9/57-11/60w; 69708 1/54-4/57.
29113 69612 3/51-5/54; 69647 7/54-12/57; 69702 4/58-3/61w.
29114 69682 3/51-6/53; 69613 8/53-1/56; 69629 4/56-8/60w.

Diagram 101:- Replacements built 1952-55.
29115 69667 6/52-11/54; 69683 12/54-3/57; 69603 10/57-7/59w.
29116 69730 6/52-5/56; 69640 8/56-11/59.
29117 69729 8/52-6/55; 69616 8/55-1/59w.
29118 69713 8/52-9/55; 69614 11/55-12/60w.
29119 69671 8/52-11/54; 69690 1/55-12/57; 69600 3/58-2/59w.
29120 69714 1/53-11/55; 69682 12/55-6/58; 69673 10/58-9/61w.
29121 69658 1/53-9/55; 69677 11/55-9/58.
29122 69609 2/53-11/55; 69723 1/56-6/59.
29123 69686 3/53-2/56; 69649 4/56-7/59w.
29124 69605 3/53-12/55; 69601 3/56-5/58w; 69726 9/58-12/60w.
29125 69669 4/53-6/55; 69633 9/55-11/57; 69721 2/58-12/60w.
29126 69707 4/53-4/56; 69622 6/56-11/59w.
29127 69711 5/53-11/56; 69603 5/57-11/60w.
29128 69644 8/53-12/55; 69732 2/56-7/59.
29129 69606 10/53-2/57; 69632 8/57-4/60.
29130 69674 12/53-2/57; 69618 5/57-9/61w.
29131 69626 4/54-9/56; 69717 12/56-1/59w.
29132 69680 8/54-1/57; 69674 4/57-6/61w.
29133 69662 2/55-7/57; 69617 9/57-7/60w.
29134 69716 2/55-2/59w; 69680 6/59-12/60w.
29135 69696 5/55-3/59.
29136 69619 7/55-2/59w.
29137 69611 8/55-10/57; 69670 12/57-9/61w.
29138 69654 8/55-4/58; 69682 7/58-12/60w.
29139 69641 9/55-12/58w.

Diagram 101:- Renumbered boilers.
29141 69632 10/53-6/57.
29142 69652 10/53-10/56; 69687 2/57-6/59.
29143 69602 2/54-7/56; 69603 11/56-8/57; 69686 9/58-9/61w.
29144 69646 5/54-11/56; 69636 2/57-11/60w.
29145 69630 6/54-12/56; 69680 3/57-5/59.
29146 69698 7/54-11/56; 69685 2/57-12/60w.

Key: n - new boiler; r - boiler renumbered; w - locomotive withdrawn.

N7 BOILER DIAGRAMS/NUMBERS

Diagram	Boiler Numbers	Remarks
30	990-1011	Eleven were saturated, of which ten were later converted to superheated. Eleven were built new with superheaters. Used on N7/GE.
98	980-989	Used on 400 series (when new) of N7/1. Had GC type circular firehole door.
98	2005-2044	Used on 800 and 900 series of N7/1. Firehole doors were dished GN type.
98	2045-2054	Used on N7/2 Nos.2632-2641.
101	2055-2086	Round-top firebox. Used on N7/3 Nos.2600-2631.
98	2087-2106	Used on N7/2 Nos.2642-2661.
30	2107-2111	Replacements for N7/GE.
98	2112-2121	Replacements for N7/1 and N7/2.
101	1950-1956	Replacements built 1932-6.
101	1957-1986	Replacements built 1941-3.
101	1930-1949	Replacements built 1945.
101	1905-1929	Replacements built 1946-8.
101	1987-1996	Replacements built 1950.
101	1890-1904	Replacements ordered in the 1950 programme and probably came out as 29100-29114.
101	29115-29139	Replacements built 1952-5.
101	29095-29099	Replacements built 1955.
101	24800-24804	Replacements built 1955-7.
98	27850-27866	Old boilers renumbered.
101	29000-29094	Old boilers renumbered.
101	29141-29146	Old boilers renumbered.

Twenty similar engines, Nos.2642 to 2661, were built from 29th June to 24th September 1927 by W. Beardmore & Co., Dalmuir but differed by having a steam brake on the engine and vacuum ejector for the train brakes, and, were the only batch built without Westinghouse brake. These and the Gorton built engines did not have controlled side traverse to the leading coupled wheels and so did not have hinged coupling rods or the square front bushes. Nos.2632 to 2661 were Part 2.

Finally, thirty-two engines, Nos.2600 to 2631, were built from 19th November 1927 to 31st December 1928 at Doncaster. These differed by having a round-top instead of a Belpaire firebox and Nos.2600 to 2609 of this batch had a different style of smokebox door with hinge straps in place of a ring. They were dual fitted for train brakes and were the first to have Group Standard buffers. Note GE pattern snifting valves were still used, and the whistle was mounted on the front of the cab instead of on the firebox as on previous batches.

This Doncaster official photograph enables some of the details to be discerned. Note gravity sanding as used throughout by all one hundred and thirty-four engines. The hand grip at the rear end of the cab, just below the roof, was fitted to those which had the built-up bunker. Westinghouse pump, where fitted, was $8/8^{1}/2$in. size on the side of smokebox, except on Nos.8000 and 8001 which had $6/6^{1}/2$in. pumps on the front end of the tank (*see* page 2, top). These engines built with round top firebox became Part 3 of the class.

Part 4 was created when No.7992 was ex-Stratford works 23rd February 1940, rebuilt with a round top firebox boiler, but it took until 30th June 1949 when No.69602 (ex-8002), was ex-works to complete the change of the twenty-two N7/GE to N7/4. These engines kept short travel valves and right hand drive. The whistle was moved from firebox to cab front but only some acquired Group Standard buffers.

CLASS N 7

8000

Stratford

To traffic 12/1914.

REPAIRS:
Str. 17/10—29/12/23.**G.**
Str. 13/7—7/10/25.**G.**
Str. 7/7—20/10/27.**G.**
Additional coal rails fitted.
Str. 12/10—14/12/29.**G.**
Superheater fitted.
Str. 30/7—24/9/31.**G.**
Str. 18/5—23/6/33.**H.**
Str. 28/6—7/7/33.**N/C.**
Str. 22/1—18/2/35.**G.**
Str. 24/10—24/11/36.**G.**
Condensing gear removed.
Str. 12/1—22/1/38.**L.**
*8/8¹/₂in. Westinghouse pump
fitted.*
Str. 28/7—26/8/38.**G.**
Str. 19/9—17/10/38.**L.**
Str. 29/9—30/11/40.**G.**
Str. 5/5—28/7/43.**G.**
Altered to N7/4.
Str. 9/9—6/10/45.**G.**
Str. 16/1—4/3/48.**G.**
Str. 25/8—30/9/50.**G.**
Str. 5—15/3/52.**N/C.**
Str. 2/1—5/2/53.**G.**
Str. 24/2—19/3/55.**C/L.**
Str. 8/8—24/9/55.**G.**
Str. 10—22/10/55.**C/L.**
Str. 11/2—22/3/58.**G.**

BOILERS:
1000.
1004 14/12/29.
 992 24/9/31.
 998 23/6/33.
 994 18/2/35.
1006 24/11/36.
 997 26/8/38.
 994 30/11/40.
2085 28/7/43.
2065 6/10/45.
1934 4/3/48.
29003 30/9/50.
29088 5/2/53.
29081 24/9/55.
29119 22/3/58.

SHED:
Stratford.

RENUMBERED:
8000 7/10/25.
7978 4/8/44.
9600 23/12/46.

ᴇ9600 4/3/48.
69600 30/9/50.

CONDEMNED: 3/2/59.
Cut up at Stratford.

8001

Stratford

To traffic 2/1915.

REPAIRS:
Str. 20/7/21—24/2/22.**G.**
Str. 19/2—9/5/24.**G.**
Str. ?/?—25/6/25.**L.**
*Ross lub. removed & replaced by
6-feed Wakefield type.*
Str. 3/6—12/11/26.**G.**
Additional coal rails fitted.
Str. 7/9—23/11/28.**G.**
Str. 9/10—7/12/29.**L.**
Str. 7/2—8/5/31.**G.**
Str. 7/1—17/2/33.**G.**
Str. 21/5—2/7/35.**G.**
Str. 6/9—7/10/36.**G.**
Condensing gear removed.
Str. 23/4—23/5/38.**G.**
*8/8¹/₂in. Westinghouse pump
fitted.*
Str. 17/3—1/4/39.**L.**
Str. 12/12/39—24/2/40.**G.**
Str. 22/4—21/5/41.**L.**
Str. 18/6—4/7/41.**L.**
Str. 11/7—15/8/42.**G.**
Str. 3/10—11/11/44.**G.**
Altered to N7/4.
Str. 16/8—5/10/46.**G.**
Str. 1—14/2/48.**L.**
Str. 12/7—11/10/48.**G.**
Str. 14/1—10/2/51.**G.**
Str. 30/9—15/10/52.**C/L.**
Str. 6/3—25/4/53.**G.**
Str. 20/10—13/11/54.**C/L.**
Str. 16/1—3/3/56.**G.**
Str. 11—28/2/58.**N/C.**

BOILERS:
1001.
 991 23/11/28.
1007 8/5/31.
1009 17/2/33.
1007 2/7/35.
1005 7/10/36.
 996 23/5/38.
1008 24/2/40.
 999 15/8/42.
2055 11/11/44.
1912 5/10/46.
1928 11/10/48.

29020 10/2/51.
29108 25/4/53.
29124 3/3/56.

SHED:
Stratford.

RENUMBERED:
8001 9/5/24.
7979 2/8/44.
9601 1/10/46.
69601 9/10/48.

CONDEMNED: 5/5/58.
Cut up at Stratford.

8002

Stratford

To traffic 6/1921.

REPAIRS:
Str. 25/1—29/3/23.**G.**
Str. 31/10/24—9/1/25.**G.**
Str. 18/2—1/6/27.**G.**
Additional coal rails fitted.
Str. 16/2—22/5/29.**G.**
Superheater & Ross 'pops' fitted.
Str. 30/5—11/8/31.**G.**
Str. 11/4—11/5/33.**G.**
Str. 19/2—21/3/35.**G.**
Str. 14/11/36—7/1/37.**G.**
Condensing gear removed.
Str. 17/8—27/9/38.**G.**
Str. 17/6—31/7/40.**G.**
Str. 23/7—15/9/42.**H/I.**
Str. 31/3—13/5/44.**G.**
Str. 15/9—20/10/46.**G.**
Str. 6—30/6/49.**G.**
Altered to N7/4.
Str. 14/8—29/9/50.**C/L.**
Str. 24/9—10/11/51.**G.**
Str. 27/1—20/2/54.**G.**
Str. 23/7—1/9/56.**G.**
Str. 20/7/59. *Not repaired.*

BOILERS:
1002.
2109 22/5/29.
 993 11/8/31.
 997 11/5/33.
 998 21/3/35.
 990 7/1/37.
1006 27/9/38.
 990 31/7/40.
2108 13/5/44.
2109 20/10/46.
2055 30/6/49.
2055 reno.29006 29/9/50.

29045 10/11/51.
29143 20/2/54.
29007 1/9/56.

SHED:
Stratford.

RENUMBERED:
8002 9/1/25.
7980 5/8/44.
9602 17/10/46.
69602 30/6/49.

CONDEMNED: 27/7/59.
Cut up at Stratford.

8003

Stratford

To traffic 6/1921.

REPAIRS:
Str. 5/4—25/5/23.**G.**
Str. 15/9/24—9/1/25.**G.**
Str. 2/9—10/12/26.**G.**
Additional coal rails fitted.
Str. 23/11/28—25/2/29.**G.**
Superheater & Ross 'pops' fitted.
Str. 28/3—21/5/30.**G.**
Str. 5/9—23/10/31.**G.**
Str. 18/7—25/8/33.**G.**
Str. 4/5—22/6/35.**G.**
Str. 3/2—15/3/37.**G.**
Condensing gear removed.
Str. 13/10—18/11/38.**G.**
Str. 1/6—9/7/40.**G.**
Altered to N7/4
Str. 27/5—5/6/42.**L.**
Str. 26/9—6/11/42.**G.**
Str. 18/2—11/4/45.**G.**
Str. 14/10—2/12/46.**G.**
Str. 24/3—7/5/49.**G.**
Str. 15/7—18/8/51.**G.**
Str. 27/10—21/11/53.**G.**
Str. 19/1—18/2/55.**C/L.**
Str. 18/1—2/2/56.**C/L.**
Str. 22/10—24/11/56.**G.**
Str. 9/8—3/10/57.**C/H.**
Str. 21/7/59. *Not repaired.*

BOILERS:
1003.
2110 25/2/29.
1006 21/5/30.
2109 23/10/31.
1008 25/8/33.
 997 22/6/35.

The fifty Part 1 engines, those originally numbered between 409 and 988, were all changed to round top firebox starting with No.826, ex-works on 8th May 1943. It took until 15th September 1956, when No.69627 (ex-460) was out for this process to be completed. Until June 1952 the rebuilt engines were designated as Part 3 but then took Part 5 to indicate they differed by still retaining short travel valves.

(centre) After the first two trial engines of 1915 which became Nos. 8000/1, the 1921 production batch had the dome placed 9in. further forward, a flatter cab roof and larger Westinghouse pump on the side of the smokebox instead of on the front end of the tank. Note 8004 still had upper lamp iron at top of smokebox. Stratford shed.

(below) Nos.990ᴇ to 999ᴇ were the last engines built at Stratford. They differed slightly from the 1921 batch in some details. Note the upper rain strip on the cab roof is shorter and only covers the entrance. The chimney lacked a brass rim and the feed pipe layout was altered. Instead of the pipe rising vertically to the dome from behind the side tank, it was arranged in front of the tank end and had two right-angle bends before reaching the clack box on the dome. King's Cross shed.

(above) The 12-element superheater boiler was taken off No.8001 in September 1928 and re-tubed to the standard 18-element. It was then used by No.7990 (July 1930 to February 1932), then No.7997 (August 1932 to August 1934), and No.7992 (October 1934 to April 1936).

Five new spare boilers, each with superheater, were built in 1928 for use on the N7/GE engines. They had Ross 'pop' safety valves.

By the early 1930's the top feed into the dome had been changed to a clack box on the side of the boiler barrel, which also eliminated the two right angle bends.

8003 cont./
2108 15/3/37.
990 18/11/38.
2085 9/7/40.
2061 6/11/42.
1931 11/4/45.
1963 2/12/46.
1961 7/5/49.
29037 18/8/51.
29009 21/11/53.
29143 24/11/56.
29115 3/10/57.

SHED:
Stratford.

RENUMBERED:
8003 9/1/25.
7981 14/8/44.
9603 23/11/46.
69603 7/5/49.

CONDEMNED: 27/7/59.
Cut up at Stratford.

_____

8004

Stratford

To traffic 6/1921.

REPAIRS:
Str. 2/1—27/2/23.**G**.
Str. 28/8—13/12/24.**G**.
Str. 6/8—30/11/26.**G**.
Additional coal rails fitted.
Str. 16/11/28—5/3/29.**G**.
Superheater fitted.
Str. 27/8—7/11/30.**G**.
Str. 30/1—4/3/32.**G**.
Str. 25/10—1/12/33.**G**.
Str. 9/7—28/8/35.**G**.
Str. 20/4—9/6/37.**G**.
Condensing gear removed.
Str. 4/2—21/3/39.**G**.
Str. 17/3—15/4/40.**L**.
Str. 23/2—31/3/41.**G**.
Altered to N7/4.
Str. 8/7—14/9/43.**G**.
Str. 22/7—7/9/45.**G**.
Str. 7/2—23/3/48.**G**.
Str. 15—16/9/49.**C/L**.
Str. 25/9—4/11/50.**G**.
Str. 29/8—12/9/52.**C/L**.
Str. 22/12/52—30/1/53.**G**.
Str. 2/9—1/10/54.**C/L**.
Str. 6/5—11/6/55.**G**.
Str. 15/9—2/11/57.**G**.
Str. 22/10—19/11/58.**C/L**.
Str. 7/8/59. *Not repaired.*

BOILERS:
1004.
1007 5/3/29.

999 7/11/30.
1004 4/3/32.
995 1/12/33.
1009 9/6/37.
2111 21/3/39.
2086 31/3/41.
2065 14/9/43.
1967 7/9/45.
1930 23/3/48.
29007 4/11/50.
29089 30/1/53.
29059 11/6/55.
29021 2/11/57.

SHED:
Stratford.

RENUMBERED:
8004 13/12/24.
7982 29/8/44.
9604 8/12/46.
69604 23/3/48.

CONDEMNED: 10/8/59.
Cut up at Stratford.

_____

8005

Stratford

To traffic 9/1921.

REPAIRS:
Str. 8/5—21/7/23.**G**.
Str. 29/1—30/4/25.**G**.
Str. 26/5—27/10/27.**G**.
Additional coal rails fitted.
Str. 25/5—31/7/29.**G**.
Superheater fitted.
Str. 5/5—10/7/31.**G**.
Str. 27/3—16/5/33.**G**.
Str. 18/12/34—25/1/35.**G**.
Str. 16/8—22/9/36.**H**.
Condensing gear removed.
Str. 12/4—11/5/38.**G**.
Str. 8/10—9/12/39.**G**.
Str. 18/2—11/4/42.**G**.
Altered to N7/4.
Str. 29/9—20/11/43.**G**.
Str. 23/1—3/3/44.**H**.
Str. 12/5—18/6/46.**G**.
Str. 12/7—28/8/48.**G**.
Str. 14/12/50—26/1/51.**G**.
Str. 22/1—5/3/53.**G**.
Str. 1/6—30/7/54.**C/L**.
Str. 19/12/55—28/1/56.**G**.
Str. 22/7—5/9/57.**C/L**.

BOILERS:
1005.
1002 31/7/29.
994 16/5/33.
1005 25/1/35.
996 22/9/36.

1010 11/5/38.
991 9/12/39.
1963 11/4/42.
1957 3/3/44.
1958 18/6/46.
1932 28/8/48.
29017 26/1/51.
29124 *(new)* 5/3/53.
29069 28/1/56.

SHED:
Stratford.

RENUMBERED:
8005 30/4/25.
7983 2/8/44.
9605 14/6/46.
69605 28/8/48.

CONDEMNED: 6/10/58.
Cut up at Stratford.

_____

8006

Stratford.

To traffic 9/1921.

REPAIRS:
Str. 6/6—1/9/23.**G**.
Str. 3/4—18/8/25.**G**.
Str. 23/6—29/10/27.**G**.
Additional coal rails fitted.
Str. 6/9—26/10/29.**G**.
Str. 11/7—2/9/31.**G**.
Superheater fitted.
Str. 29/5—14/7/33.**G**.
Str. 11—16/8/34.**L**.
Str. 7/3—6/4/35.**G**.
Str. 24/10—3/12/36.**G**.
Condensing gear removed.
Str. 15—26/10/37.**L**.
Str. 7/6—1/7/38.**G**.
Str. 16—28/9/38.**L**.
Str. 28/1—9/3/40.**G**.
Str. 8/2—31/3/42.**G**.
Altered to N7/4.
Str. 30/4—10/6/44.**G**.
Str. 23/6—19/8/46.**G**.
Str. 8/10—11/11/47.**L**.
Str. 2/5—3/6/49.**G**.
Str. 4/6—11/8/51.**G**.
Str. 10—28/3/53.**C/L**.
Str. 14/9—10/10/53.**G**.
Str. 14—16/10/53.**N/C**.
Str. 9—14/8/54.**C/L**.
Str. 2/11/55—11/1/56.**C/H**.
Str. 11/2—16/3/57.**G**.

BOILERS:
1006.
1005 26/10/29.
991 2/9/31.
1002 14/7/33.

1011 6/4/35.
2107 3/12/36.
999 1/7/38.
996 9/3/40.
1962 31/3/42.
1963 10/6/44.
1964 19/8/46.
1978 3/6/49.
29036 11/8/51.
29129 *(new)* 10/10/53.
29011 16/3/57.

SHED:
Stratford.

RENUMBERED:
8006 18/8/25.
7984 29/8/44.
9606 14/8/46.
69606 3/6/49.

CONDEMNED: 11/8/58.
Cut up at Stratford.

_____

8007

Stratford.

To traffic 10/1921.

REPAIRS:
Str. 2/4—1/6/23.**G**.
Str. 31/10/24—8/1/25.**G**.
Str. 4/11/26—12/3/27.**G**.
Additional coal rails fitted.
Str. 22/6—28/9/28.**G**.
Str. 19/7—26/9/30.**G**.
Superheater fitted.
Str. 25/7—5/9/32.**G**.
Str. 10/5—14/6/34.**G**.
Str. 20/12/35—28/1/36.**G**.
Str. 6/8—9/9/37.**G**.
Condensing gear removed
Str. 3/5—24/6/39.**G**.
Str. 26/7—20/9/41.**G**.
Altered to N7/4.
Str. 6/2—10/3/44.**G**.
Str. 17/4—18/5/46.**G**.
Str. 12/7—4/9/48.**G**.
Str. 3/11/50—20/1/51.**G**.
Str. 15/4—22/5/53.**G**.
Str. 13—21/8/53.**N/C**.
Str. 24/10—3/12/55.**G**.

BOILERS:
1007.
1009 28/9/28.
1011 26/9/30.
1006 5/9/32.
999 14/6/34.
1003 28/1/36.
992 9/9/37.
993 24/6/39.
2079 20/9/41.

The chimney with brass rim on Nos.8000 to 8011, gradually gave way to the plain cast type. From 31st July to 6th September 1944 Nos. 8000-11 were changed to 7978 to 7989 to clear the way for new 350h.p. diesel shunters to be numbered from 8000 in Thompson's scheme.

Between 12th November 1926 (No.8001) and 31st January 1929 (No.868) the twenty-two N7/GE, and the N7/1, built with three open coal rails on the bunker, had them effectively closed by the fitting of three additional similar rails, to help prevent spillage of small coal. No.968, which had been fitted with an experimental bunker (*see* page 31, bottom), was brought into line in January 1934.

From June 1928 to July 1930 Nos.8000 to 8011 had a large ventilator provided in the wooden roof of the cab. Note the toolbox on the right hand tank, the only N7 noted as being so equipped (*see* also page 15, middle).

Beginning in March 1933, Nos.8002 to 8011 and 7990 to 7999 changed from wood cab roof to a new steel one, with a single curved full length rain strip. The new roof was slightly lower and had a shallow cut-out above the entrance.

Nos.8000 and 8001 (69600 and 69601 later), also changed to steel cab roof but kept the higher arched profile. On No.69601 there was a slight cut-out above cab entrance but on No.9600 (*see* page 70, middle) the edge was straight all the way across.

8007 cont./
1958 10/3/44.
1968 18/5/46.
1979 4/9/48.
29106 20/1/51.
29102 22/5/53.
29035 3/12/55.

SHED:
Stratford.

RENUMBERED:
8007 8/1/25.
7985 14/8/44.
9607 16/5/46.
69607 4/9/48.

CONDEMNED: 22/7/58.
Cut up at Stratford.

8008

Stratford.

To traffic 10/1921.

REPAIRS:
Str. 26/2—11/5/23.**G.**
Str. 5/12/24—12/2/25.**G.**
Str. 14/1—27/5/27.**G.**
Additional coal rails fitted.
Str. 23/2—21/5/29.**G.**
Sup.and Ross 'pops' fitted.
Str. 27/8—7/11/30.**G.**
Str. 16/8—4/10/32.**G.**
Str. 19/7—28/8/34.**G.**
Str. 1—30/3/36.**G.**
Str. 17/10—10/11/37.**G.**
Condensing gear removed.
Str. 28/4—12/5/38.**L.**
Str. 27/6—19/8/39.**G.**
Str. 31/1—19/3/42.**G.**
Altered to N7/4.
Str. 13/8—16/9/44.**G**
Str. 25/7—12/9/46.**G.**
Str. 30/3—7/7/48.**G.**
Str. 21/12/50—27/1/51.**G.**
Str. 20—23/8/52.**C/L.**
Str. 3/2—6/3/53.**C/L.**
Str. 4/5—4/6/53.**G.**
Str. 3—7/5/54.**C/L.**
Str. 19/6—25/8/56.**G.**

BOILERS:
1008.
2111 21/5/29.
1011 4/10/32.
1010 28/8/34.
991 30/3/36.
2109 10/11/37.
995 19/8/39.
2078 19/3/42.
2080 16/9/44.
1911 12/9/46.
2085 7/7/48.
29019 27/1/51.
29093 4/6/53.
29083 25/8/56.

SHED:
Stratford.

RENUMBERED:
8008 12/2/25.
7986 31/7/44.
9608 6/9/46.
69608 3/7/48.

CONDEMNED: 11/8/58.
Cut up at Stratford.

8009

Stratford.

To traffic 10/1921.

REPAIRS:
Str. 17/8—7/11/23.**G.**
Str. 18/7—30/10/25.**G.**
Str. 24/2—5/6/28.**G.**
Superheater and additional coal rails fitted.
Str. 17/5—14/8/30.**G.**
Str. 30/5—1/7/32.G.
Str. 1/3—5/4/34.**G.**
Str. 3/9—10/10/35.**G.**
Str. 2/4—14/5/37.**G.**
Condensing gear removed.
Str. 9/12/38—24/1/39.**G.**
Str. 27/3—12/4/40.**L.**
Str. 1/1—28/2/41.**G.**
Str. 13/8—16/10/43.**G.**
Str. 25/11—15/12/45.**G.**
Str. 6/3—1/4/47.**L.**
Str. 23/4—31/7/47.**L.**
Str. 22/6—21/8/48.**G.**
Altered to N7/4.
Str. 10/4—2/5/50.**C/L.**
Str. 16/11—22/12/50.**G.**
Str. 20/1—14/2/53.**G.**
Str. 19/1—5/2/55.**C/L.**
Str. 14/11—30/12/55.**G.**
Str. 7—22/2/57.**C/L.**

BOILERS:
1009.
2107 5/6/28.
2110 1/7/32.
1003 5/4/34.
1009 10/10/35.
2111 14/5/37.
998 24/1/39.
997 28/2/41.
992 16/10/43.
2111 15/12/45.
1911 21/8/48.
29015 22/12/50.
29122 *(new)* 14/2/53.
29102 30/12/55.

SHED:
Stratford.

RENUMBERED:
8009 30/10/25.
7987 29/8/44.
9609 22/12/46.
69609 21/8/48.

CONDEMNED: 28/4/58.
Cut up at Stratford.

8010

Stratford.

To traffic 11/1921.

REPAIRS:
Str. 21/7—3/10/23.**G.**
Str. 2/6—3/9/25.**G.**
Str. 10/6—13/10/27.**G.**
Additional coal rails fitted.
Str. 10/8—5/10/29.**G.**
Superheater fitted.
Str. 4/7—5/9/31.**G.**
Str. 19/6—26/7/33.**G.**
Str. 13/3—18/4/35.**G.**
Str. 29/12/36—2/2/37.**G.**
Condensing gear removed.
Str. 30/8—14/10/38.**G.**
Str. 8—27/12/39.**G.**
Str. 14/9—3/12/40.**G.**
Str. 1/8—5/10/43.**G.**
Altered to N7/4.
Str. 18/10—17/11/45.**G.**
Str. 6/1—28/2/48.**G.**
Str. 21/7—26/8/50.**G.**
Str. 8—9/9/50.**N/C.**
Str. 7/1—21/2/53.**G.**
Str. 10/11—24/12/55.**G.**
Str. 26/9—6/11/57.**C/L.**
Str. 4—7/3/58.**C/L.**

BOILERS:
1010.
1008 5/10/29.
1007 26/7/33.
2108 18/4/35.
994 2/2/37.
992 3/12/40.
1953 5/10/43.
2085 17/11/45.
1939 28/2/48.
1996 26/8/50.
29068 21/2/53.
29061 24/12/55.

SHED:
Stratford.

RENUMBERED:
8010 3/9/25.
7988 6/9/44.
9610 22/12/46.
E9610 28/2/48.
69610 26/8/50.

CONDEMNED: 1/1/59.
Cut up at Stratford.

8011

Stratford.

To traffic 11/1921.

REPAIRS:
Str. 23/8—10/11/23.**G.**
Str. 27/6—22/10/25.**G.**
Str. 22/7—5/11/27.**G.**
Additional coal rails fitted.
Str. 13/9—5/11/29.**G.**
Superheater fitted.
Str. 15/8—9/10/31.**G.**
Str. 27/6—11/8/33.**G.**
Str. 3/4—8/5/35.**G.**
Str. 2—22/5/36.**L.**
Str. 17/11—24/12/36.**G.**
Condensing gear removed.
Str. 6/7—4/8/38.**G.**
Str. 3/3—23/4/40.**G.**
Altered to N7/4.
Str. 18/12/41—2/1/42.**L.**
Str. 30/8—3/10/42.**G.**
Str. 24/11—2/12/42.**L.**
Str. 15/11—16/12/44.**G.**
Str. 22/12/46—1/2/47.**G.**
Str. 8/9—27/10/48.**H.**
Str. 16/12/49—14/1/50.**G.**
Str. 26/11—5/1/52.**C/L.**
Str. 10/9—24/10/52.**G.**
Str. 24—25/2/54.**C/L.**
Str. 8—26/11/54.**C/L.**
Str. 14/6—6/8/55.**G.**
Str. 23/8—14/9/55.**N/C.**
Str. 10/1—8/2/57.**C/L.**
Str. 28/10—30/11/57.**G.**
Str. 14/1—19/2/60.**C/L.**

WORKS CODES:- Cw - Cowlairs. Dar- Darlington. Don - Doncaster. Ghd - Gateshead. Gor - Gorton. Inv - Inverurie. Str - Stratford.
REPAIR CODES:- **C/H** - Casual Heavy. **C/L** - Casual Light. **G** - General. **H**- Heavy. **H/I** - Heavy Intermediate. **L** - Light. **L/I** - Light Intermediate. **N/C** - Non-Classified.

Along with the cab roof change, a single sunken footstep was inserted into the side of the bunker. At the rear end of the cab, almost at roof level, a hand grip was fitted.

Between January 1935 and February 1938 the whole class had condensing equipment removed, but they retained the tank vent pipes near to the cab.

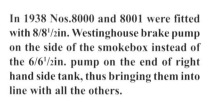

In 1938 Nos.8000 and 8001 were fitted with 8/8$^{1}/_{2}$in. Westinghouse brake pump on the side of the smokebox instead of the 6/6$^{1}/_{2}$in. pump on the end of right hand side tank, thus bringing them into line with all the others.

Except on the first five engines, the upper lamp iron was fitted on the smokebox door, and by the 1930's Nos.8000 to 8004 had been brought into line (*see* page 15, middle and page 16, middle).

All were fitted for carrying GER type destination boards. At the front the brackets were fitted on the upper half of the smokebox door, and on the back of the bunker they were just below the coal rails (*see* page 19, top). Also, compare this view with that on page 13.

8011 cont./
BOILERS:
 1011.
 1003 5/11/29.
 993 11/8/33.
 990 8/5/35.
 1007 24/12/36.
 2107 4/8/38.
 2061 23/4/40.
 2064 3/10/42.
 2066 16/12/44.
 1931 1/2/47.
 1952 14/1/50.
 1952 reno.29053 5/1/52.
 29082 24/10/52.
 29137 *(new)* 6/8/55.
 29027 30/11/57.

SHED:
Stratford.

RENUMBERED:
 8011 22/10/25.
 7989 29/8/44.
 9611 6/1/47.
 69611 23/10/48.

CONDEMNED: 24/11/60.
Cut up at Stratford.

___

7990

Stratford.

To traffic 15/12/23.

REPAIRS:
Str. 19/11/25—26/1/26.**G.**
Str. 16/3—22/6/28.**G.**
Additional coal rails fitted.
Str. 10/5—25/7/30.**G.**
Str. 13/2—21/3/32.**G.**
Str. 28/6—17/8/33.**H.**
Str. 20/7—26/9/34.**G.**
Str. 4/6—9/7/36.**G.**
Condensing gear removed.
Str. 24/11—18/12/37.**G.**
Str. 16—25/11/38.**L.**
Str. 6—21/4/39.**L.**
Str. 7/9—7/10/39.**G.**
Str. 3/8—5/9/41.**G.**
Str. 16/9—2/10/42.**L.**
Str. 16/12/43—25/1/44.**G.**
Altered to N7/4
Str. 25/11—21/12/44.**L.**
Str. 23/10—24/11/45.**G.**
Str. 10/5—30/6/46.**L.**
Str. 24/7—3/9/48.**G.**
Str. 22/2—31/3/51.**G.**
Str. 6—21/1/53.**N/C.**
Str. 24/5—2/7/54.**G.**
Str. 29/7/59. *Not repaired.*

BOILERS:
 990.
 1001 25/7/30.
 1005 21/3/32.
 996 26/9/34.
 1004 9/7/36.
 2110 18/12/37.
 1002 7/10/39.
 998 5/9/41.
 2086 25/1/44.
 1965 24/11/45.
 1942 3/9/48.
 29113 *(new)* 31/3/51.
 29046 2/7/54.

SHEDS:
Ardsley.
Stratford 11/7/24.
Neasden 5/5/25.
Stratford 16/11/25.
Parkeston 12/12/48.
Stratford 27/7/52.
Hornsey 10/6/56.
Colchester 30/6/57.

RENUMBERED:
 990E *as built.*
 7990 26/1/26.
 9612 5/1/47.
 69612 3/9/48.

CONDEMNED: 3/8/59.
Cut up at Stratford.

___

7991

Stratford.

To traffic 1/1/24.

REPAIRS:
Str. 14/1—25/3/26.**G.**
Str. 21/1—28/4/27.**G.**
Str. 28/4—22/8/28.**G.**
Additional coal rails fitted.
Str. 12/7—15/10/30.**G.**
Str. 15/8—24/9/32.**G.**
Str. 26/6—16/8/34.**G.**
Str. 5—24/1/36.**L.**
Str. 16/6—20/7/36.**G.**
Condensing gear removed.
Str. 5/3—7/4/38.**G.**
Str. 24/11/39—17/1/40.**G.**
Str. 23/10—2/12/41.**G.**
Altered to N7/4.
Str. 24/3—13/5/44.**G.**
Str. 18/9—13/10/45.**G.**
Str. 28/8—14/10/46.**G.**
Str. 11/9—22/10/49.**G.**
Str. 20/9—21/10/50.**C/L.**
Str. 5—9/2/52.**N/C.**
Str. 14—28/2/52.**C/L.**
Str. 20/7—15/8/53.**G.**
Str. 20/1—3/3/56.**G.**

Str. 30/6—21/7/58.**C/L.**

BOILERS:
 991.
 995 22/8/28.
 996 15/10/30.
 2107 16/8/34.
 999 20/7/36.
 1008 7/4/38.
 1010 17/1/40.
 1952 2/12/41.
 1961 13/5/44.
 1943 13/10/45.
 1908 22/10/49.
 1908 reno.29012 21/10/50.
 29114 15/8/53.
 29077 3/3/56.

SHEDS:
Bradford.
Stratford 7/7/24.
Neasden 5/5/25.
Stratford 31/12/25.
Hatfield 2/12/49.
Colwick 29/4/51.
Hatfield 4/11/51.
Stratford 22/11/53.
Colchester 29/9/57.
Parkeston 1/11/59.

RENUMBERED:
 991E *as built.*
 7991 25/3/26.
 9613 3/1/47.
 69613 22/10/49.

CONDEMNED: 9/11/59.
Cut up at Stratford.

___

7992

Stratford.

To traffic 1/1/24.

REPAIRS:
Str. 22/1—31/3/26.**G.**
Str. 9/3—9/6/28.**G.**
Additional coal rails fitted.
Str. 2/8—31/10/30.**G.**
Str. 23/8—8/10/32.**G.**
Str. 6/9—5/10/34.**G.**
Str. 26/4—29/5/36.**G.**
Condensing gear removed.
Str. 9/1—21/2/38.**G.**
Str. 16/12/39—23/2/40.**G.**
Altered to N7/4.
Str. 31/5—18/7/42.**G.**
Str. 29/9—10/11/44.**G.**
Str. 10/5—27/6/46.**G.**
Str. 6/1—3/3/49.**G.**
Str. 25/2—4/4/52.**G.**
Str. 7—29/10/54.**C/L.**
Str. 19/9—3/11/55.**G.**

Str. 19/4—10/6/60.**C/H.**

BOILERS:
 992.
 1009 31/10/30.
 990 8/10/32.
 1001 5/10/34.
 1010 29/5/36.
 1004 21/2/38.
 2064 23/2/40.
 1964 18/7/42.
 1978 27/6/46.
 1976 3/3/49.
 29060 4/4/52.
 29118 3/11/55.

SHEDS:
King's Cross.
Hitchin 23/6/24.
Neasden 7/5/25.
Stratford 31/12/25.
Parkeston 10/4/49.
Stratford 19/8/51.

RENUMBERED:
 992E *as built.*
 7992 31/3/26.
 9614 20/6/46.
 69614 3/3/49.

CONDEMNED: 4/12/60.
Cut up at Stratford.

___

7993

Stratford.

To traffic 8/1/24.

REPAIRS:
Str. 24/12/25—18/3/26.**G.**
Str. 9/3—30/6/28.**G.**
Additional coal rails fitted.
Str. 7/6—5/9/30.**G.**
Str. 4/8—9/9/32.**G.**
Str. 14/8—11/9/34.**G.**
Str. 18/2—13/3/36.**G.**
Str. 28/9—22/10/37.**G.**
Condensing gear removed.
Str. 23—29/6/38.**L.**
Str. 4/6—28/7/39.**G.**
Str. 10—21/3/41.**L.**
Str. 21/9—22/10/41.**G.**
Str. 2/9—6/11/43.**G.**
Str. 22/5—23/6/45.**G.**
Altered to N7/4.
Str. 17—28/1/47.**L.**
Str. 10/4—2/9/47.**L.**
Str. 18/3—29/5/48.**G.**
Str. 24/4—25/5/49.**H/I.**
Str. 1/3—5/4/52.**G.**
Str. 3/2—18/3/54.**C/L.**
Str. 25/4—21/5/55.**G.**
Str. 15/3—25/4/56.**C/L.**

7993 cont./
Str. 1/9/60. *Not repaired.*

BOILERS:
993.
997 5/9/30.
2108 9/9/32.
2110 11/9/34.
2109 13/3/36.
1003 22/10/37.
2111 22/10/41.
2070 23/6/45.
1967 29/5/48.
29061 5/4/52.
29055 21/5/55.

SHEDS:
King's Cross.
Hatfield 23/6/24.
Stratford 9/12/25.
Parkeston 12/12/48.
Stratford 10/4/49.
Hatfield 2/12/49.
Colwick 29/4/51.
Hatfield 21/3/54.
Stratford 4/4/54.
Hornsey 10/6/56.
Lowestoft 23/6/57.
Stratford 7/12/58.
King's Lynn 26/7/59.
Stratford 9/8/59.

RENUMBERED:
993E *as built.*
7993 18/3/26.
9615 5/1/47.
69615 29/5/48.

CONDEMNED: 12/9/60.
Cut up at Stratford.

_____

7994

Stratford.

To traffic 16/1/24.

REPAIRS:
Str. 11/12/25—25/2/26.**G.**
Str. 12/3—4/7/28.**G.**
Additional coal rails.
Str. 21/6—18/9/30.**G.**
Str. 5/7—18/8/32.**G.**
Str. 4/6—12/7/34.**G.**
Str. 8/3—4/4/36.**G.**
Str. 5/10—3/11/37.**G.**
Condensing gear removed.
Str. 23/7—12/9/39.**G.**
Str. 25/12/41—10/2/42.**G.**
Altered to N7/4.
Str. 19—26/2/42.**N/C.**
Str. 11/8—28/9/44.**G.**
Str. 24/11/46—5/1/47.**G.**
Str. 31/7—3/9/49.**G.**

Str. 3/6—25/7/52.**G.**
Str. 15/9—7/10/54.**C/L.**
Str. 14/6—13/8/55.**G.**
Str. 23/5—27/6/57.**C/L.**

BOILERS:
994
1010 18/8/32.
1004 12/7/34.
2110 4/4/36.
1002 3/11/37.
2109 12/9/39.
2066 10/2/42.
1952 28/9/44.
2059 5/1/47.
1973 3/9/49.
29073 25/7/52.
29117 13/8/55.

SHEDS:
King's Cross.
Hatfield 28/5/24.
Stratford 27/11/25.
Cambridge 10/2/57.

RENUMBERED:
994E *as built.*
7994 25/2/26.
9616 16/12/46.
69616 3/9/49.

CONDEMNED: 1/1/59.
Cut up at Stratford.

_____

7995

Stratford.

To traffic 23/1/24.

REPAIRS:
Str. 24/12—18/3/26.**G.**
Str. 10/4—20/7/28.**G.**
Additional coal rails
Str. 31/1—29/8/30.**G.**
Str. 21/6—12/8/32.**G.**
Str. 26/3—4/5/34.**G.**
Str. 22/10—15/11/35.**G.**
Str. 8/6—8/7/37.**G.**
Condensing gear removed.
Str. 15/11—10/12/37.**L.**
Str. 21/3—3/5/39.**G.**
Str. 10/1—6/3/41.**G.**
Str. 9/12—29/1/43.**L.**
Str. 18/3—29/4/44.**G.**
Altered to N7/4.
Str. 3/1—2/2/46.**G.**
Str. 5/10—9/11/48.**G.**
Str. 13/9—13/10/51.**G.**
Str. 26/5—24/6/53.**C/L.**
Str. 22/9—23/10/54.**G.**
Str. 25/7—28/9/57.**G.**
Str. 27/5—10/6/59.**C/L.**
Str. 30/6/60. *Not repaired.*

BOILERS:
995.
996 20/7/28.
990 29/8/30.
2107 12/8/32.
2109 4/5/34.
992 15/11/35.
993 8/7/37.
1009 3/5/39.
2108 6/3/41.
1986 29/4/44.
1961 2/2/46.
1965 9/11/48.
29042 13/10/51.
29027 23/10/54.
29133 28/9/57.

SHEDS:
King's Cross.
Hatfield 21/6/24.
Stratford 10/12/25.
Hatfield 26/10/52.
Stratford 22/11/53.
Cambridge 10/2/57.
King's Lynn 9/3/58.
Stratford 30/11/58.
Colchester 14/12/58.
Stratford 6/12/59.

RENUMBERED:
995E *as built.*
7995 18/3/26.
9617 3/1/47.
69617 6/11/48.

CONDEMNED: 4/7/60.
Cut up at Stratford.

_____

7996

Stratford.

To traffic 31/1/24.

REPAIRS:
Str. 18/12/25—5/3/26.**G.**
Str. 24/3—13/7/28.**G.**
Additional coal rails.
Str. 10/5—15/7/30.**G.**
Str. 26/9—27/11/31.**G.**
Str. 10/10—9/11/33.**G.**
Str. 4/7—16/8/35.**G.**
Str. 31/3—13/5/37.**G.**
Condensing gear removed.
Str. 5/7—18/8/38.**G.**
Str. 16/5—22/6/40.**G.**
Str. 7/6—21/7/42.**G.**
Str. 17/9—21/10/44.**G.**
Str. 19/5—26/6/46.**G.**
Str. 28/5—7/7/48.**G.**
Altered to N7/4.
Str. 11/2—10/3/51.**G.**
Str. 13—24/5/52.**C/L.**
Str. 9/9—10/10/53.**G.**

Str. 31/3—6/5/54.**C/L.**
Str. 2—5/11/54.**C/L.**
Str. 8—28/1/55. *Not repaired.*
Str. 8/4—17/5/57.**G.**
Str. 17—27/8/59.**C/L.**

BOILERS:
996.
997 13/7/28.
2110 15/7/30.
995 27/11/31.
992 9/11/33.
2111 16/8/35.
997 13/5/37.
1007 18/8/38.
999 22/6/40.
2109 21/7/42.
2107 26/6/46.
2065 7/7/48.
29023 10/3/51.
29002 10/10/53.
29130 17/5/57.

SHEDS:
Bradford.
Stratford 25/6/24.
Neasden 5/5/25.
Stratford 3/12/25.
Hornsey 20/11/55.
Hatfield 1/2/59.
King's Cross 1/1/61.
Stratford 16/4/61.

RENUMBERED:
996E *as built.*
7996 5/3/26.
9618 20/6/46.
69618 3/7/48.

CONDEMNED: 10/9/61.
Cut up at Stratford.

_____

7997

Stratford.

To traffic 16/2/24.

REPAIRS:
Str. 14/1—25/3/26.**G.**
Str. 5/4—6/7/28.**G.**
Additional coal rails.
Str. 5/7—25/9/30.**G.**
Str. 5/7—26/8/32.**G.**
Str. 16/8—7/9/34.**G.**
Str. 21/5—15/6/35.**H.**
Str. 21/4—23/5/36.**G.**
Condensing gear removed.
Str. 10—27/8/37.**L.**
Str. 2—29/1/38.**G.**
Str. 2/10—25/11/39.**G.**
Str. 2/1—17/2/42.**G.**
Altered to N7/4.
Str. 9/7—19/8/44.**G.**

Some with the taller GER type chimney were later changed to 'plant pot' type which was 4¼in. shorter. Nos.69602, 69608, 69614, 69617, 69618, 69620 and 69621 were recorded as so altered.

Although the twenty-two N7/GE engines had cut-out toe hole at the cab entrance, provision of the facility was missed on the engines built after 1923.

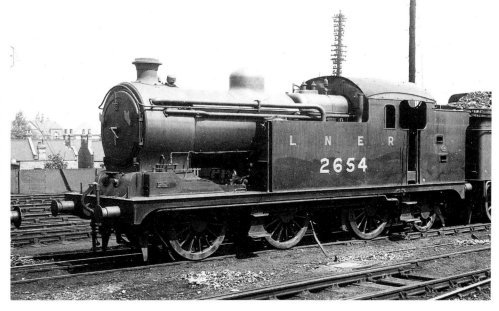

The toe hole was duly put in later on the other one hundred and twelve. The twenty, Nos.2642 to 2661, which came from Beardmore had a circular cover around the base of the safety valves, the only ones so equipped. Hornsey shed.

These safety valve base covers were gradually discarded, or drifted to other engines (*see* page 33, top) due to boiler transfers.

The built-up bunker on the Part 2 engines had the back plate arc-shaped at the top, in contrast to those with rails, as those were level across the back.

(below) Bunkers on Part 3 engines were similar to Part 2 and also had arc-shaped top to back plate. This view is the left side of the Doncaster official shown on page 12.

7997 cont./
Str. 6/10—11/11/46.**G.**
Str. 22/3—30/4/49.**G.**
Str. 3/1—3/2/50.**C/L.**
Str. 5/5—6/6/52.**G.**
Str. 30/4—7/5/54.**C/L.**
Str. 17/2—2/3/55.**C/L.**
Str. 3/6—23/7/55.**G.**
Str. 24/3—2/5/58.**C/L.**

BOILERS:
997.
2108 6/7/28.
1001 26/8/32.
1006 7/9/34.
1008 23/5/36.
991 29/1/38.
2110 25/11/39.
2055 17/2/42.
2059 19/8/44.
2055 11/11/46.
2074 30/4/49.
29069 6/6/52.
29136 *(new)* 23/7/55.

SHEDS:
Bradford.
Stratford 3/7/24.
Neasden 5/5/25.
Stratford 3/12/25.
Parkeston 12/12/48.
Stratford 10/4/49.
Colchester 20/11/55.
Stratford 4/3/56.
Cambridge 10/2/57.
King's Lynn 8/6/58.
Stratford 30/11/58.

RENUMBERED:
997E *as built.*
7997 25/3/26.
9619 2/11/46.
69619 30/4/49.

CONDEMNED: 16/2/59.
Cut up at Stratford.

7998

Stratford.

To traffic 16/2/24.

REPAIRS:
Str. 24/12/25—19/3/26.**G.**
Str. 10/2—9/5/28.**G.**
Additional coal rails.
Str. 25/4—28/7/30.**G.**
Str. 7/5—24/6/32.**G.**
Str. 20/3—26/4/34.**G.**
Str. 12/12/35—21/1/36.**G.**
Str. 1/8—4/9/37.**G.**
Condensing gear removed.
Str. 28/3—6/4/39.**L.**

Str. 13/6—18/8/39.**G.**
Str. 1/6—4/7/40.**H.**
Str. 23/1—7/3/42.**G.**
Str. 17/10—24/11/44.**G.**
Str. 18/6—27/8/47.**G.**
Altered to N7/4.
Str. 17/6—1/7/49.**C/L.**
Str. 7/8—8/9/50.**G.**
Str. 10/2—19/3/55.**G.**
Str. 4/8—7/9/57.**G.**
Str. 8—24/12/59.**N/C.**

BOILERS:
998.
1010 28/7/30.
999 24/6/32.
991 26/4/34.
1002 21/1/36.
995 4/9/37.
992 18/8/39.
2107 4/7/40.
2110 7/3/42.
2066 27/8/47.
29000 8/9/50.
29021 19/3/55.
29112 7/9/57.

SHEDS
Stratford.
Parkeston 12/12/48.
Stratford 4/12/49.
Hatfield 30/12/49.
Colwick 29/4/51.
Stratford 11/4/54.
Cambridge 10/2/57.
King's Lynn 8/6/58.
Stratford 1/3/59.

RENUMBERED:
998E *as built.*
7998 19/3/26.
9620 2/1/47.
69620 1/7/49.

CONDEMNED: 24/11/60.
Cut up at Stratford.

7999

Stratford.

To traffic 19/3/24.

REPAIRS:
Str. 22/1—31/3/26.**G.**
Str. 17/3—17/8/28.**G.**
Additional coal rails.
Str. 26/7—12/9/30.**G.**
Str. 1/9—7/10/32.**G.**
Str. 20/4—31/5/35.**G.**
Str. 14/3—3/5/37.**G.**
Condensing gear removed.
Str. 14—20/1/38.**L.**
Str. 1/11—9/12/38.**G.**

Str. 23/7—21/9/40.**G.**
Str. 10—19/3/42.**L.**
Str. 4—27/5/42.**H.**
Str. 15/8—6/11/43.**G.**
Str. 27/1—26/2/46.**G.**
Altered to N7/4.
Str. 21/7—19/8/47.**G.**
Str. 30/11/48—11/1/49.**G.**
Str. 7/1—16/2/52.**G.**
Str. 26/1—10/3/56.**G.**
Str. 26/1—6/2/59.**C/L.**
Str. 18/12/59—11/3/60.**G.**

BOILERS:
999.
998 12/9/30.
2111 7/10/32.
993 31/5/35.
998 3/5/37.
2108 9/12/38.
1006 21/9/40.
2107 27/5/42.
1969 26/2/46.
2078 19/8/47.
1968 11/1/49.
29056 16/2/52.
29071 10/3/56.
29086 11/3/60.

SHEDS:
Stratford.
Neasden 5/5/25.
Stratford 16/11/25.
Parkeston 12/12/48.
Stratford 19/8/51.
Colwick 6/7/52.
Woodford 25/1/53.
Colwick 31/5/53.
Stratford 11/4/54.
Lowestoft 24/2/57.
Stratford 30/8/59.

RENUMBERED:
999E *as built.*
7999 31/3/26.
9621 2/1/47.
69621 8/1/49.

WITHDRAWN: 11/9/62.
Purchased for preservation.

409

Gorton .

To traffic 30/8/25.

REPAIRS:
Str. 18/8—30/11/27.**G.**
Additional coal rails.
Str. 6/9—2/11/29.**G.**
Str. 27/8—16/10/31.**G.**
Str. 14/9—16/10/33.**G.**
Str. 3—27/9/35.**G.**

Str. 30/5—13/7/37.**G.**
Condensing gear removed.
Str. 16/1—14/3/39.**G.**
Str. 25/1—10/3/41.**G.**
Str. 16/6—23/7/42.**G.**
Str. 27/11/43—7/1/44.**G.**
Altered to N7/5.
Str. 26/4—26/5/45.**G**
Str. 30/7—10/9/47.**G.**
Str. 17/8—14/9/50.**G.**
Str. 9/2—7/3/53.**G.**
Str. 12/11—2/12/54.**C/L.**
Str. 19/7—3/9/55.**C/L.**
Str. 7/5—16/6/56.**G.**
Str. 25/11—21/12/57.**C/L.**

BOILERS:
980.
2096 16/10/31.
986 16/10/33.
2120 27/9/35.
2103 13/7/37.
2118 14/3/39.
2037 10/3/41.
1977 7/1/44.
1936 26/5/45.
1950 10/9/47.
29001 14/9/50.
29091 7/3/53.
29126 16/6/56.

SHEDS:
Gorton.
King's Cross 13/10/25.
Stratford 6/8/27.

RENUMBERED:
9622 20/10/46.
69622 14/9/50.

CONDEMNED: 24/11/59.
Cut up at Stratford.

421

Gorton.

To traffic 27/9/25.

REPAIRS:
Str. 1/9—24/11/27.**G.**
Additional coal rails.
Str. 17/8—19/10/29.**G.**
Str. 25/7—19/9/31.**G.**
Str. 7/9—6/10/33.**G.**
Str. 31/8—8/10/35.G.
Str. 23/5—6/7/37.**G.**
Condensing gear removed.
Str. 25/4—1/6/39.**G.**
Str. 13/7—16/8/41.**G.**
Str. 28/6—29/7/42.**L.**
Str. 4—17/12/42.**L.**
Str. 23/1—23/2/44.**G.**
Str. 21/4—30/5/46.**G.**

421 cont./
Str. 21/11—24/12/48.**G.**
Str. 18—25/1/51.**C/L.**
Str. 19/5—26/6/52.**G.**
Altered to N7/5.
Str. 27/5—6/6/53.**C/L.**
Str. 26/9—11/11/55.**G.**
Str. 14—29/3/57.**C/L.**
Str. 28/5—5/6/58.**C/L.**

BOILERS:
 981.
 2020 19/9/31.
 2095 6/10/33.
 2088 8/10/35.
 2031 6/7/37.
 2115 1/6/39.
 2091 16/8/41.
 2047 23/2/44.
 2045 30/5/46.
 2089 24/12/48.
 2089 reno.27852 25/1/51.
 29071 26/6/52.
 29025 11/11/55.

SHEDS:
Gorton.
King's Cross 13/10/25.
Stratford 22/8/27.

RENUMBERED:
 9623 30/11/46.
 69623 24/12/48.

CONDEMNED: 12/2/59.
Cut up at Stratford.

_____

426

Gorton.

To traffic 10/10/25.

REPAIRS:
Str. 26/5—29/8/28.**G.**
Additional coal rails.
Str. 5/7—19/9/30.**G.**
Str. 10/5—13/6/32.**G.**
Str. 21/9—15/11/34.**G.**
Str. 19/7—26/8/36.**G.**
Condensing gear removed.
Str. 26/4—26/5/38.**G.**
Str. 22/11/38—6/1/39.**L.**
Str. 11/2—20/3/40.**G.**
Str. 16/11—19/12/41.**G.**
Str. 15/6—29/7/44.**G.**
Str. 11/8—23/9/46.**G.**
Str. 18/9—15/10/49.**G.**
Str. 4—19/11/49.**C/L.**
Str. 25/8—9/9/50.**C/L.**
Str. 24/11/52—2/1/53.**G.**
Str. 25/10—17/12/55.**G.**
Altered to N7/5.
Str. 27/11/58. *Not repaired.*

BOILERS:
 982.
 2037 13/6/32.
 2050 15/11/34.
 2090 26/8/36.
 2049 26/5/38.
 2097 20/3/40.
 2028 19/12/41.
 2114 29/7/44.
 2051 23/9/46.
 2088 15/10/49.
 2088 reno.27850 9/9/50.
 27865 2/1/53.
 29057 17/12/55.

SHEDS:
Gorton.
Hatfield 20/10/25.
Stratford 28/11/28.

RENUMBERED:
 9624 20/7/46.
 69624 15/10/49.

CONDEMNED: 1/12/58.
Cut up at Stratford.

_____

456

Gorton.

To traffic 24/10/25.

REPAIRS:
Str. 7/6—5/9/28.**G.**
Additional coal rails.
Str. 13/9—31/10/30.**G.**
Str. 12/1—23/2/33.**G.**
Str. 27/8—12/10/34.**G.**
Str. 2—29/7/36.**G.**
Condensing gear removed.
Str. 23/12/37—27/1/38.**G.**
Str. 29/6—9/7/38.**H.**
Str. 15/10—18/11/39.**G.**
Str. 22/1—8/2/40.**L.**
Str. 20/2—9/3/40.**L.**
Str. 1/2—13/3/42.**G.**
Str. 23/7—26/8/44.**G.**
Str. 20/7—9/9/47.**G.**
Str. 7—23/12/48.**L.**
Str. 23/11/49—11/2/50.**G.**
Altered to N7/5.
Str. 2/9—14/10/52.**G.**
Str. 6—15/12/54.**C/L.**
Str. 5/9—21/10/55.**G.**
Str. 11—14/3/57.**N/C.**

BOILERS:
 983.
 2032 31/10/30.
 2091 23/2/33.
 2106 29/7/36.
 2087 27/1/38.
 2089 9/7/38.

2014 18/11/39.
2024 13/3/42.
2094 9/9/47.
2076 11/2/50.
2076 reno.29080 14/10/52.
29062 21/10/55.

SHEDS:
Gorton.
Hornsey 20/10/25.
Stratford 17/12/28.

RENUMBERED:
 9625 17/10/46.
 69625 23/12/48.

CONDEMNED: 17/4/59.
Cut up at Stratford.

_____

457

Gorton.

To traffic 31/10/25.

REPAIRS:
Str. 12/4—28/6/28.**G.**
Additional coal rails.
Str. 26/10—12/12/30.**G.**
Str. 12/3—15/4/32.**G.**
Str. 4/6—13/7/34.**G.**
Str. 2—31/1/36.**G.**
Str. 2/9—6/10/37.**G.**
Condensing gear removed.
Str. 2/8—21/9/39.**G.**
Str. 15/2—11/4/42.**G.**
Str. 6/8—28/9/44.**G.**
Str. 28/11/46—10/1/47.**G.**
Str. 28/5—2/7/49.**G.**
Str. 2/8—8/9/51.**G.**
Str. 27/11—8/12/51.**N/C.**
Str. 5—9/2/52.**N/C.**
Str. 22/2—3/4/54.**G.**
Altered to N7/5.
Str. 14/9—20/10/56.**G.**
Str. 13—20/1/58.**C/L.**
Str. 4/6/59 *Not repaired.*

BOILERS:
 984.
 983 12/12/30.
 2040 15/4/32.
 2046 13/7/34.
 986 31/1/36.
 984 6/10/37.
 2117 21/9/39.
 2014 11/4/42.
 2054 28/9/44.
 2118 10/1/47.
 2087 2/7/49.
 27858 8/9/51.
 29131 *(new)* 3/4/54.
 29056 20/10/56.

SHEDS:
Gorton.
Hatfield 6/11/25.
King's Cross 11/9/28.
Hatfield 15/4/29.
Hornsey 4/3/30.
Stratford 12/12/30.

RENUMBERED:
 9626 21/7/46.
 69626 2/7/49.

CONDEMNED: 8/6/59.
Cut up at Stratford.

_____

460

Gorton.

To traffic 14/11/25.

REPAIRS:
Str. 24/1—14/4/28.**G.**
Additional coal rails.
Str. 7/6—29/8/30.**G.**
Str. 27/3—2/5/34.**G.**
Str. 12/11—10/12/35.**G.**
Str. 15—27/1/36.**L.**
Str. 17/8—13/9/37.**G.**
Condensing gear removed.
Str. 14/5—17/6/39.**G.**
Str. 10/8—19/9/41.**G.**
Str. 4/8—2/10/43.**G.**
Str. 3/1—2/2/46.**G.**
Str. 1/12/48—3/1/49.**G.**
Str. 4/6—10/8/51.**G.**
Str. 8/1—6/2/54.**G.**
Str. 21/12/54—3/2/55.**C/L.**
Str. 26/5—30/6/55.**C/L.**
Str. 8/8—15/9/56.**G.**
Altered to N7/5.
Str. 7—20/1/58.**C/L.**

BOILERS:
 985.
 981 2/5/34.
 2087 10/12/35.
 2007 13/9/37.
 2040 17/6/39.
 2012 19/9/41.
 2011 2/2/46.
 2097 3/1/49.
 27854 10/8/51.
 27866 6/2/54.
 29048 15/9/56.

SHEDS:
Gorton.
Hatfield 27/11/25.
Stratford 21/1/28.

RENUMBERED:
 9627 20/7/46.
 69627 1/1/49.

460 cont./
CONDEMNED: 23/3/59.
Cut up at Stratford.

_____

464

Gorton.

To traffic 21/11/25.

REPAIRS:
Str. 2/9—25/11/27.**G.**
Additional coal rails.
Str. 23/11/29—23/1/30.**G.**
Str. 21/11/32—13/1/33.**G.**
Str. 31/12/34—15/2/35.**G.**
Str. 17/10—18/11/36.**G.**
Condensing gear removed.
Str. 24/7—24/8/38.**G.**
Str. 1/6—5/7/40.**G.**
Str. 20/8—28/9/42.**G.**
Str. 26/11/44—6/1/45.**G.**
Str. 21/9—11/11/47.**G.**
Str. 15/7—25/8/51.**G.**
Altered to N7/5.
Str. 9/4—18/5/56.**G.**
Str. 27/11/58 *Not repaired.*

BOILERS:
986.
2118 13/1/33.
2025 18/1/36.
988 24/8/38.
2023 5/7/40.
2038 28/9/42.
2092 11/11/47.
29039 25/8/51.
29016 18/5/56.

SHEDS:
Gorton.
King's Cross 4/12/25.
Stratford 20/8/27.

RENUMBERED:
9628 2/1/47.
69628 25/8/51.

CONDEMNED: 1/12/58.
Cut up at Stratford.

_____

471

Gorton.

To traffic 28/11/25.

REPAIRS:
Str. 1/9—24/11/27.**G.**
Additional coal rails.
Str. 7/12/29—8/2/30.**G.**
Str. 5/3—13/5/32.**G.**
Str. 29/5—29/6/34.**G.**

Str. 4/2—6/3/36.**G.**
Str. 29/9—25/10/37.**G.**
Condensing gear removed.
Str. 10/5—30/6/39.**G.**
Str. 14/9—14/10/41.**G.**
Str. 14/11—24/12/43.**G.**
Str. 20/12/45—12/1/46.**G.**
Str. 5/10—11/11/48.**G.**
Str. 7—8/12/50.**C/L.**
Str. 8/9—16/10/52.**G.**
Str. 17/2—12/3/55.**C/L.**
Str. 12/3—20/4/56.**G.**
Altered to N7/5.
Str. 30/10—18/11/59.**N/C.**
Str. 15/8/60. *Not repaired.*

BOILERS:
987.
2104 13/5/32.
2045 29/6/34.
981 6/3/36.
2044 25/10/37.
2047 30/6/39.
2013 14/10/41.
2119 24/12/43.
2023 12/1/46.
2106 11/11/48.
27861 16/10/52.
29114 20/4/56.

SHEDS:
Gorton.
King's Cross 4/12/25.
Stratford 20/8/27.
Hornsey 25/12/55.
Hatfield 22/3/59.

RENUMBERED:
9629 27/7/46.
69629 6/11/48.

CONDEMNED: 29/8/60.
Cut up at Stratford.

_____

473

Gorton.

To traffic 28/11/25.

REPAIRS:
Str. 12/8—12/11/27.**G.**
Str. 6/9—2/11/29.**G.**
Additional coal rails.
Str. 8/8—9/10/31.**G.**
Str. 23/10—17/11/33.**G.**
Str. 29/10—27/11/35.**G.**
Str. 5/10—4/11/37.**G.**
Condensing gear removed.
Str. 7/11—20/12/39.**G.**
Str. 4/4—12/5/42.**G.**
Str. 27/8—14/10/44.**G.**
Str. 16/3—23/4/47.**G.**
Str. 2/6—21/7/50.**G.**

Altered to N7/5.
Str. 17/5—19/6/54.**G.**
Str. 24/12/56—26/1/57.**G.**
Str. 5—8/3/57.**N/C.**
Str. 8—16/8/58.**C/L.**
Str. 22/2—25/3/60.**C/L.**
Str. 30/3—8/4/60.**N/C.**

BOILERS:
988.
981 9/10/31.
989 17/11/33.
2097 27/11/35.
986 4/11/37.
2089 20/12/39.
2092 12/5/42.
2115 14/10/44.
2053 23/4/47.
1991 21/7/50.
29145 19/6/54.
29127 26/1/57.

SHEDS:
Gorton.
King's Cross 9/12/25.
Stratford 6/8/27.

RENUMBERED:
9630 25/7/46.
69630 21/7/50.

CONDEMNED: 24/11/60.
Cut up at Stratford.

_____

475

Gorton.

To traffic 11/12/25.

REPAIRS:
Str. 17/3—1/6/28.**G.**
Additional coal rails.
Str. 6/1—27/6/29.**G.**
Str. 20/9—7/11/30.**G.**
Str. 23/1—27/2/32.**G.**
Str. 21/9—19/10/33.**G.**
Str. 12/8—12/9/35.**G.**
Str. 2/5—9/6/37.**G.**
Condensing gear removed.
Str. 25/1—2/3/39.**G.**
Str. 27/2—5/4/41.**G.**
Str. 12/12/43—15/1/44.**G.**
Str. 31/3—6/5/46.**G.**
Str. 24/3—7/5/49.**G.**
Str. 18—28/5/49.**N/C.**
Str. 3/6—2/8/52.**G.**
Str. 23/8—1/9/54.**C/L.**
Str. 21/2—19/3/55.**G.**
Altered to N7/5.
Str. 19/12/57—25/1/58.**G.**
Str. 12—18/8/60.**N/C.**
Str. 16/1/61 *Not repaired.*

BOILERS:
989.
2025 7/11/30.
2026 27/2/32.
2011 19/10/33.
2031 12/9/35.
2024 9/6/37.
2046 2/3/39.
2025 5/4/41.
2013 15/1/44.
2087 6/5/46.
2045 7/5/49.
27859 2/8/52.
29096 *(new)* 19/3/55.
29000 25/1/58.

SHEDS:
Gorton.
Hatfield 29/12/25.
Stratford 10/12/28.
Hatfield 11/4/54.
King's Cross 1/1/61.

RENUMBERED:
9631 30/4/46.
69631 7/5/49.

CONDEMNED: 23/1/61.
Cut up at Stratford.

_____

826

Gorton.

To traffic 19/1/26.

REPAIRS:
Str. 2/12/27—13/3/28.**G.**
Additional coal rails.
Str. 4/5—30/7/30.**G.**
Str. 19/5—19/7/32.**G.**
Str. 14/10—2/12/32.**L.**
Str. 23/10—4/12/34.**G.**
Str. 27/9—23/10/36.**G.**
Condensing gear removed.
Str. 21/8—30/9/38.**G.**
Str. 17—23/11/38.**L.**
Str. 28/7—26/9/40.**G.**
Str. 28/2—8/5/43.**G.**
Altered to N7/5.
Str. 3—29/6/45.**G.**
Str. 9—29/3/47.**L.**
Str. 16/10—9/12/47.**G.**
Str. 19/11—17/12/49.**C/L.**
Str. 12/11—22/12/50.**G.**
Str. 25/8—3/10/53.**G.**
Str. 6—15/4/54.**C/L.**
Str. 9/4—11/5/56.**C/L.**
Str. 11/6—2/8/57.**G.**
Str. 25/4—12/8/60.**C/H.**

BOILERS:
2005.
2029 19/7/32.

The first ten built at Doncaster had their style of smokebox door which was more dished than the Stratford design. It also had long hinge straps set closer together, instead of a circular steel ring. A knob was provided which did not feature on GE type doors.

That GN style door did not gain Stratford's approval and from No.2610 to 2631 Doncaster turned them out with the GE style door.

The ten GN style doors on Nos.2600 to 2609 (9702 to 9711 later), were replaced by GE pattern and no photograph later than 1937 of No.2605 with hinge straps has been located.

In 1929 ten spare Belpaire boilers were built to ease interchanging. They had Ross 'pop' valves and had alternative feed points either through the dome or on the firebox back plate. The dome cover was then adapted to suit.

From August 1926 to December 1933, No.968 had an experimental bunker to try and reduce coal spillage. It was the only one so altered as the addition of three extra coal rails was cheaper and proved sufficiently effective.

826 cont./
2006 4/12/34.
2100 23/10/36.
2050 30/9/38.
985 26/9/40.
2083 8/5/43.
1939 29/6/45.
1918 9/12/47.
29107 22/12/50.
29141 3/10/53.
29129 2/8/57.
29077 12/8/60.

SHEDS:
Gorton.
Stratford 4/2/26.
Hatfield 21/12/49.
King's Cross 25/7/54.
Hatfield 15/8/54.
King's Cross 1/1/61.
Stratford 16/4/61.

RENUMBERED:
9632 12/12/46.
69632 22/12/50.

CONDEMNED: 16/9/62.
Cut up at Stratford.

_____

827

Gorton.

To traffic 2/2/26.

REPAIRS:
Str. 20/1—5/4/28.**G.**
Additional coal rails.
Str. 10/5—3/7/30.**G.**
Str. 19/3—29/4/32.**G.**
Str. 10/5—13/6/34.**G.**
Str. 18/1—25/2/36.**G.**
Str. 3—30/10/37.**G.**
Condensing gear removed.
Str. 6/8—29/9/39.**G.**
Str. 27/9—28/10/41.**G.**
Str. 13/5—1/7/44.**G.**
Altered to N7/5.
Str. 3/8—5/10/46.**G.**
Str. 7/7—27/8/49.**G.**
Str. 18/9—27/10/51.**G.**
Str. 5—15/12/51.**N/C.**
Str. 4/9—10/10/53.**G.**
Str. 28/7—3/9/55.**G.**
Str. 4/11—5/12/57.**G.**
Str. 31/7/59 *Not repaired.*

BOILERS:
2006.
2119 29/4/32.
2112 13/6/34.
2105 25/2/36.
2034 30/10/37.
2044 29/9/39.

2115 28/10/41.
1960 1/7/44.
1910 5/10/46.
2072 27/8/49.
29046 27/10/51.
29012 10/10/53.
29125 3/9/55.
24804 *(new)* 5/12/57.

SHEDS:
Gorton.
Stratford 25/2/26.

RENUMBERED:
9633 26/9/46.
69633 27/8/49.

CONDEMNED: 10/8/59.
Cut up at Stratford.

_____

828

Gorton.

To traffic 12/2/26.

REPAIRS:
Str. 27/1—20/4/28.**G.**
Additional coal rails.
Str. 10/5—14/7/30.**G.**
Str. 8/8—24/9/32.**G.**
Str. 14/8—2/10/34.**G.**
Str. 7/8—8/9/36.**G.**
Condensing gear removed.
Str. 10/7—18/8/38.**G.**
Str. 14/7—4/9/40.**G.**
Str. 20/2—3/4/43.**G.**
Str. 25/5—14/7/45.**G.**
Str. 24/2—11/5/48.**G.**
Str. 31/12/50—2/2/51.**G.**
Altered to N7/5.
Str. 8—18/4/52.**C/L.**
Str. 4/5—6/6/53.**G.**
Str. 8/10—10/11/56.**G.**

BOILERS:
2007.
2010 24/9/32.
2008 2/10/34.
2005 8/9/36.
983 18/8/38.
988 4/9/40.
2049 3/4/43.
2030 14/7/45.
2033 11/5/48.
29018 2/2/51.
29110 6/6/53.
29010 10/11/56.

SHEDS:
Gorton.
Stratford 25/2/26.

RENUMBERED:
9634 11/8/46.
69634 8/5/48.

CONDEMNED: 13/1/59.
Cut up at Stratford.

_____

829

Gorton.

To traffic 26/2/26.

REPAIRS:
Str. 11/11/27—9/2/28.**G.**
Additional coal rails.
Str. 28/12/29—27/2/30.**G.**
Str. 2/1—20/2/32.**G.**
Str. 30/1—1/3/34.**G.**
Str. 3—28/10/35.**G.**
Str. 13/6—21/7/37.**G.**
Condensing gear removed.
Str. 20/3—2/5/39.**G.**
Str. 30/5—19/6/40.**L.**
Str. 3/5—11/6/41.**G.**
Str. 15/10—7/11/41.**L.**
Str. 26/12/43—12/2/44.**G.**
Altered to N7/5.
Str. 3—16/9/44.**L.**
Str. 22/7—7/9/46.**G.**
Str. 21/1—9/3/49.**G.**
Str. 4/2—1/3/52.**G.**
Str. 12/1—7/2/53.**C/L.**
Str. 8/9—15/10/55.**G.**

BOILERS:
2008.
2045 20/2/32.
2113 1/3/34.
2019 28/10/35.
2117 21/7/37.
2101 2/5/39.
2051 11/6/41.
1980 12/2/44.
1954 7/9/46.
1955 9/3/49.
29057 1/3/52.
29082 15/10/55.

SHEDS:
Gorton.
Stratford 26/3/26.
Parkeston 10/4/49.
Stratford 27/7/52.
Hatfield 22/11/53.

RENUMBERED:
9635 30/8/46.
69635 9/3/49.

CONDEMNED: 9/3/59.
Cut up at Stratford.

_____

830

Gorton.

To traffic 12/3/26.

REPAIRS:
Str. 5/4—27/7/28.**G.**
Str. 4/6—29/8/30.**G.**
Str. 30/9—28/10/32.**G.**
Str. 11/10—20/11/34.**G.**
Str. 6/3—17/4/36.**G.**
Condensing gear removed.
Str. 29/12/37—26/1/38.**G.**
Str. 5/9—7/10/39.**G.**
Str. 31/8—3/10/41.**G.**
Str. 23/8—11/9/42.**L.**
Str. 12/4—13/5/44.**G.**
Altered to N7/5.
Str. 9/3—1/5/47.**G.**
Str. 17/9—21/10/50.**G.**
Str. 23/11—19/12/53.**G.**
Str. 17/1—23/2/57.**G.**
Str. 8—22/9/58.**C/L.**
Str. 19/2—18/3/60.**C/L.**

BOILERS:
2009.
2014 28/10/32.
2028 20/11/34.
2089 17/4/36.
2022 26/1/38.
2102 7/10/39.
2103 3/10/41.
1950 13/5/44.
1951 1/5/47.
29103 *(new)* 21/10/50.
29011 19/12/53.
29144 23/2/57.

SHEDS:
Gorton.
Stratford 30/3/26.

RENUMBERED:
9636 10/8/46.
69636 21/10/50.

CONDEMNED: 24/11/60.
Cut up at Stratford.

_____

832

Gorton.

To traffic 31/3/26.

REPAIRS:
Str. 3/2—28/4/28.**G.**
Additional coal rails.
Str. 5/4—30/5/30.**G.**
Str. 7/6—20/7/32.**G.**
Str. 12/6—1/8/34.**G.**

From late 1926 the fitting of the three additional coal rails proceeded as quickly as the seventy-two engines went to works for normal repair.

From December 1933 all had their wood cab roof replaced by a steel one on which was a single curved rain strip. At the same time, a single sunken footstep was cut into the side of the bunker on the GE and on forty-five of the fifty Part 1 engines.

Between January and July 1935 the last five Part 1 engines, Nos. 866, 867, 868, 870 and 873 had two footsteps inserted on both sides of their bunker. Curiously these differed from the arrangement on Parts 2 and 3 in that the upper step was to the rear of the lower one, compare with the view of No.2607 on page 34, bottom.

From No.2642, ex-works 5th January 1935 to No.918 ex-works 16th February 1938, all had the condensing gear taken off, although the tank vent pipes remained.

No.2607 a Part 3 engine with a wooden roof to the cab and a straight rain strip, also still with condensing gear which 2607 had until going to works 6th September 1936. Note GS buffers fitted.

832 cont./
Str. 21/5—9/7/36.**G.**
Condensing gear removed.
Str. 6/4—4/5/38.**G.**
Str. 9/11—7/12/38.**L.**
Str. 24/2—6/4/40.**G.**
Str. 5—28/2/42.**L.**
Str. 1/4—22/5/42.**G.**
Str. 11/10—24/11/44.**G.**
Str. 27/9—20/11/47.**G.**
Str. 11/12/49—28/1/50.**G.**
Str. 11/11—24/12/52.**G.**
Str. 29/8—29/10/55.**G.**
Altered to N7/5.

BOILERS:
2010.
2036 20/7/32.
983 1/8/34.
2035 9/7/36.
2020 4/5/38.
2121 6/4/40.
2099 22/5/42.
2098 24/11/44.
2027 20/11/47.
2054 28/1/50.
27864 24/12/52.
29073 29/10/55.

SHEDS:
Gorton.
Stratford 28/4/26.
Staveley 15/7/51.
Stratford 9/12/51.
Hatfield 11/4/54.
Hornsey 18/5/58.

RENUMBERED:
9637 11/8/46.
69637 28/1/50.

CONDEMNED: 31/3/59.
Cut up at Stratford.

_____

833

Gorton.

To traffic 16/4/26.

REPAIRS:
Str. 16/3—9/6/28.**G.**
Additional coal rails.
Str. 3/5—27/6/30.**G.**
Str. 30/4—13/6/31.**G.**
Str. 26/7—16/9/32.**G.**
Str. 14/6—10/8/34.**G.**
Str. 21/5—26/6/36.**G.**
Condensing gear removed.
Str. 16/2—25/3/38.**G.**
Str. 6/1—15/2/40.**G.**
Str. 23/3—11/4/41.**L.**
Str. 14/6—28/7/42.**G.**
Str. 12/11/44—6/1/45.**G.**

Str. 8/5—20/6/47.**G.**
Str. 4/12/49—7/1/50.**G.**
Altered to N7/5.
Str. 25/3—1/5/53.**G.**
Str. 25/3—5/5/56.**G.**

BOILERS:
2011.
2114 27/6/30.
2116 16/9/32.
2020 26/6/36.
2027 25/3/38.
2019 15/2/40.
2009 28/7/42.
2094 6/1/45.
2054 20/6/47.
2063 7/1/50.
29015 1/5/53.
29104 5/5/56.

SHEDS:
Gorton.
Stratford 28/4/26.
Colwick 22/4/51.
Hatfield 4/11/51.
King's Cross 25/7/54.
Hatfield 5/9/54.

RENUMBERED:
9638 4/5/46.
69638 7/1/50.

CONDEMNED: 19/5/59.
Cut up at Stratford.

_____

834

Gorton.

To traffic 30/4/26.

REPAIRS:
Str. 5/4—13/7/28.**G.**
Additional coal rails.
Str. 21/6—5/9/30.**G.**
Str. 22/8—7/10/32.**G.**
Str. 19/7—22/8/34.**G.**
Str. 7/5—13/6/36.**G.**
Condensing gear removed.
Str. 27/2—30/3/38.**G.**
Str. 4—13/5/39.**L.**
Str. 3/2—16/3/40.**G.**
Str. 5—16/1/41.**L.**
Str. 11/5—5/6/41.**L.**
Str. 14—18/6/42. *Not repaired.*
Str. 16/10—27/11/42.**G.**
Str. 22/4—26/5/45.**G.**
Str. 30/11/47—10/1/48.**G.**
Altered to N7/5.
Str. 15/3—13/4/48.**L.**
Str. 19/2—8/4/50.**G.**
Str. 3—31/10/52.**G.**
Str. 27/5—3/7/53.**G.**
Str. 10/2—17/3/56.**G.**

Str. 24/6—24/7/57.**C/L.**
Str. 20/8—13/9/57.**C/L.**

BOILERS:
2012.
2028 7/10/32.
985 22/8/34.
2029 13/6/36.
2023 30/3/38.
987 16/3/40.
2035 27/11/42.
2020 26/5/45.
1922 10/1/48.
1922 reno.29083 31/10/52.
29020 3/7/53.
29079 17/3/56.

SHEDS:
Gorton.
Stratford 15/7/26.
Hatfield 21/12/49.

RENUMBERED:
9639 19/8/46.
69639 10/4/48.

CONDEMNED: 5/1/59.
Cut up at Stratford.

_____

837

Gorton.

To traffic 1/6/26.

REPAIRS:
Str. 28/4—20/7/28.**G.**
Additional coal rails.
Str. 17/10—7/12/29.**L.**
Str. 9/8—16/10/30.**G.**
Str. 1/10—18/11/32.**G.**
Str. 2/9—9/11/34.**G.**
Str. 9/7—13/8/36.**G.**
Condensing gear removed.
Str. 3/6—1/7/38.**G.**
Str. 23/8—22/9/39.**L.**
Str. 26/5—27/6/40.**G.**
Str. 1—7/8/42.**L.**
Str. 19/12/42—26/2/43.**G.**
Str. 6/5—8/6/45.**G.**
Str. 28/12/47—4/3/48.**G.**
Str. 25/6—12/8/50.**G.**
Altered to N7/5.
Str. 10/11—12/12/53.**G.**
Str. 10/12/54—22/1/55.**C/L.**
Str. 25/3—19/4/56.**C/L.**
Str. 30/5—24/8/56.**C/H.**
New chimney.
Str. 29/4—31/5/57.**L/I.**
Str. 5/11/59—4/2/60.**G.**

BOILERS:
2013.
2007 18/11/32.

2047 9/11/34.
983 13/8/36.
985 1/7/38.
2096 27/6/40.
2095 26/2/43.
2033 8/6/45.
2022 4/3/48.
1993 12/8/50.
29014 12/12/53.
29116 24/8/56.
24801 4/2/60.

SHEDS:
Gorton.
Stratford 15/7/26.
Hatfield 29/12/49.
King's Cross 1/1/61.
Stratford 9/4/61.

RENUMBERED:
9640 10/5/46.
ᴇ**9640** 4/3/48.
69640 12/8/50.

CONDEMNED: 16/9/62.
Cut up at Stratford.

_____

838

Gorton.

To traffic 23/6/26.

REPAIRS:
Str. 4/5—27/7/28.**G.**
Additional coal rails.
Str. 21/6—11/9/30.**G.**
Str. 11/8—22/9/32.**G.**
Str. 30/8—15/10/34.**G.**
Str. 25/7—28/8/36.**G.**
Condensing gear removed.
Str. 5/5—3/6/38.**G.**
Str. 14/1—16/2/40.**G.**
Str. 18/3—8/5/42.**G.**
Str. 8/10—9/11/44.**G.**
Str. 1/6—3/7/47.**G.**
Str. 22/1—25/3/50.**G.**
Str. 5/8—6/9/52.**G.**
Altered to N7/5.
Str. 12/8—10/9/55.**G.**
Str. 11/6—25/7/57.**C/L.**
Str. 27/11/58 *Not repaired.*

BOILERS:
2014.
2033 22/9/32.
2036 15/10/34.
2042 28/8/36.
2114 3/6/38.
2015 16/2/40.
2093 8/5/42.
2120 9/11/44.
2116 3/7/47.
29078 6/9/52.

35

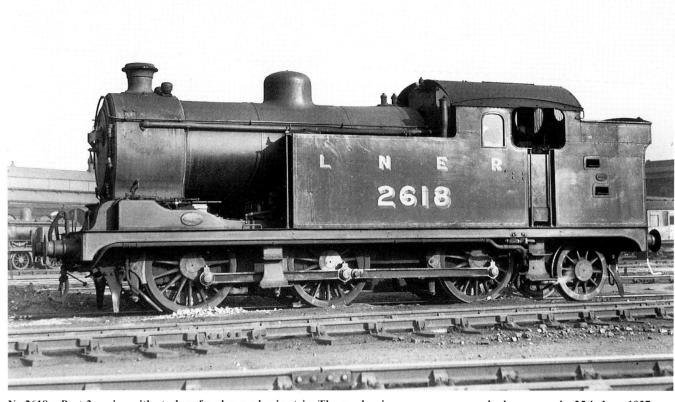

No.2618 a Part 3 engine with steel roof and curved rain strip. The condensing gear was removed when ex-works 25th June 1937.

838 cont./
29139 *(new)* 10/9/55.

SHEDS:
Gorton.
Stratford 15/7/26.

RENUMBERED:
9641 20/8/46.
69641 25/3/50.

CONDEMNED: 1/12/58.
Cut up at Stratford.

_____

850

Gorton.

To traffic 16/7/26.

REPAIRS:
Str. 10/3—13/6/28.**G.**
Additional coal rails.
Str. 19/7—3/10/30.**G.**
Str. 22/12/32—9/2/33.**G.**
Str. 10/1—16/2/35.**G.**
Str. 14/3—23/4/37.**G.**
Condensing gear removed.
Str. 14/5—26/6/39.**G.**
Str. 8/3—4/5/42.**G.**
Addl washout plugs fitted.

Str. 17/12/44—2/2/45.**G.**
Str. 3—28/4/47.**L.**
Str. 15/3—23/6/48.**G.**
Str. 11/2—10/3/51.**G.**
Altered to N7/5.
Str. 29/11/54—8/1/55.**G.**
Str. 30/6—15/8/58.**G.**
Str. 26/8—2/9/58.**N/C.**
Str. 30/5—23/7/60.**C/L.**

BOILERS:
2015.
2011 3/10/30.
2015 9/2/33.
2039 16/2/35.
2094 23/4/37.
2116 26/6/39.
2102 4/5/42.
2089 2/2/45.
2102 23/6/48.
29022 10/3/51.
29005 8/1/55.
29034 15/8/58.

SHEDS:
Gorton.
King's Cross 12/8/26.
Stratford 11/12/28.
King's Lynn 8/10/50.
Stratford 29/10/50.

RENUMBERED:
9642 10/5/46.
69642 19/6/48.

CONDEMNED: 24/11/60.
Cut up at Stratford.

_____

851

Gorton.

To traffic 31/7/26.

REPAIRS:
Str. 17/10—24/12/27.**G.**
Str. 4/1—1/3/30.**G.**
Additional coal rails.
Str. 7/1—20/2/32.**G.**
Str. 12/5—22/6/35.**G.**
Str. 11/4—26/5/37.**G.**
Condensing gear removed.
Str. 12/7—19/8/39.**G.**
Str. 7/6—17/7/42.**G.**
Str. 26/11/44—22/1/45.**G.**
Str. 25/6—18/8/47.**G.**
Str. 29/6—21/8/48.**H.**
Str. 18/6—29/7/50.**G.**
Altered to N7/5.
Str. 8/4—2/5/53.**G.**
Str. 8/2—17/3/56.**G.**
Str. 18—27/3/57.**N/C.**

BOILERS:
2016.
2031 20/2/32.
2052 22/6/35.
2039 26/5/37.
2007 19/8/39.
2043 17/7/42.
2117 22/1/45.
2115 18/8/47.
1992 29/7/50.
29104 2/5/53.
29017 17/3/56.

SHEDS:
Gorton.
King's Cross 12/8/26.
Stratford 15/10/27.
Staveley 15/7/51.
Stratford 9/12/51.

RENUMBERED:
9643 6/10/46.
69643 21/8/48.

CONDEMNED: 19/5/58.
Cut up at Stratford.

_____

GER design parallel case buffers with hollow spindle and circular flange were the original fitting on all except the Part 3 engines built at Doncaster. Many still had this type to withdrawal.

Some buffer type changes did occur. Ex-works 22nd May 1929, No.8002 had GS buffers (*see* page 16, middle) but at a subsequent date it had parallel shank type again but with rectangular flange.

When replacement buffers were needed it was usual to fit GS type. No.69647 had been so fitted at least by 2nd July 1948 and possibly much earlier.

From 8th May 1943 on No.826 the Belpaire firebox boiler was replaced by a round-top type and these had hand holes instead of washout plugs. No.9636 (ex 830) was so fitted from 13th May 1944 and all Part 1 engines were changed.

852

Gorton.

To traffic 31/8/26.

REPAIRS:
Str. 8/6—14/9/28.**G.**
Additional coal rails.
Str. 23/8—31/10/30.**G.**
Str. 3/11—2/12/32.**G.**
Str. 28/11/34—21/1/35.**G.**
Str. 5/1—15/2/37.**G.**
Condensing gear removed.
Str. 26/3—12/5/39.**G.**
Str. 16/12/41—30/1/42.**G.**
Str. 29/5—2/6/42.**L.**
Str. 10/12/44—12/1/45.**G.**
Str. 16/11/47—6/1/48.**G.**
Str. 4—25/11/49.**C/L.**
Str. 7/5—10/6/50.**G.**
Altered to N7/5.
Str. 1/7—14/8/53.**G.**
Str. 18/12/55—28/1/56.**G.**

BOILERS:
2017.
2009 2/12/32.
2014 21/1/35.
2048 15/2/37.
2043 12/5/39.
2101 30/1/42.
2043 12/1/45.
2048 6/1/48.
1988 10/6/50.
29128 *(new)* 14/8/53.
29101 28/1/56.

SHEDS:
Gorton.
King's Cross 28/9/26.
Stratford 29/11/28.
Hatfield 9/12/49.

RENUMBERED:
9644 6/12/46.
69644 10/6/50.

CONDEMNED: 27/1/59.
Cut up at Stratford.

_____

853

Gorton.

To traffic 17/9/26.

REPAIRS:
Str. 5/7—16/10/28.**G.**
Additional coal rails.
Str. 6/9—13/11/30.**G.**
Str. 15/5—23/6/33.**G.**
Str. 4—31/7/35.**G.**
Str. 19/7—28/8/37.**G.**

Condensing gear removed.
Str. 16/8—30/9/39.**G.**
Str. 7—30/5/41.**L.**
Str. 16/7—26/8/42.**G.**
Str. 18—27/3/43.**L.**
Str. 3/12/44—13/1/45.**G.**
Str. 28/8—4/11/47.**G.**
Str. 26/1—15/4/50.**G.**
Str. 27/10—29/11/52.**G.**
Str. 7—21/4/54.**C/L.**
Str. 19/4—14/5/55.**G.**
Altered to N7/5.
Str. 1—16/4/57.**C/L.**
Str. 4/9—5/10/57.**G.**
Str. 5—8/2/60.**N/C.**
Str. 10/2—17/3/60.**C/L.**

BOILERS:
2018.
2097 23/6/33.
2015 31/7/35.
2052 28/8/37.
2048 30/9/39.
2089 26/8/42.
2036 13/1/45.
2099 4/11/47.
27863 29/11/52.
29038 14/5/55.
29090 5/10/57.

SHEDS:
Gorton.
King's Cross 26/10/26.
Stratford 19/10/28.

RENUMBERED:
9645 22/8/46.
69645 15/4/50.

CONDEMNED: 1/11/60.
Cut up at Stratford.

_____

865

Gorton.

To traffic 9/10/26.

REPAIRS:
Str. 17/8—9/11/28.**G.**
Additional coal rails.
Str. 30/8—31/10/30.**G.**
Str. 23/1—23/2/33.**G.**
Str. 28/12/33—25/1/34.**L.**
Str. 23/1—8/3/35.**G.**
Str. 30/9—30/10/36.**G.**
Condensing gear removed.
Str. 23/7—23/8/38.**G.**
Str. 3/9—28/10/40.**G.**
Str. 14/4—28/6/43.**G.**
Str. 17/6—28/7/45.**G.**
Str. 19/7—21/9/48.**G.**
Str. 15/7—25/8/51.**G.**
Str. 12—16/5/52.**C/L.**

Str. 15/5—12/6/53.**C/L.**
Str. 2/4—29/5/54.**G.**
Rebuilt to N7/5.
Str. 26/4—11/5/56.**C/L.**
Str. 25/11—29/12/56.**G.**
Str. 27/7—22/10/59.**G.**

BOILERS:
2019.
984 23/2/33.
2012 8/3/35.
980 30/10/36.
2026 23/8/38.
2045 28/10/40.
2096 28/6/43.
2044 28/7/45.
2030 21/9/48.
27856 25/8/51.
29144 29/5/54.
29009 29/12/56.
29087 22/10/59.

SHEDS:
Gorton.
Stratford 27/10/26.
Cambridge 1/6/36.
Stratford 5/6/38.
Cambridge (Bishops Stortford)
1/6/38.
Stratford 5/6/38.

RENUMBERED:
9646 20/7/46.
69646 18/9/48.

CONDEMNED: 16/9/62.
Cut up at Stratford.

_____

866

Gorton.

To traffic 29/10/26.

REPAIRS:
Str. 7/9/28—3/1/29.**G.**
Additional coal rails.
Str. 2/5—23/7/31.**G.**
Str. 6/6—21/7/33.**G.**
Str. 4/6—11/7/35.**G.**
Str. 3/2—19/3/37.**G.**
Condensing gear removed.
Str. 24/12/38—9/2/39.**G.**
Str. 16/11—26/12/40.**G.**
Str. 20—27/5/42.**L.**
Str. 28/9—20/11/43.**G.**
Altered to N7/5.
Str. 28/2—3/4/46.**G.**
Str. 16/5—2/7/48.**G.**
Str. 18/8—22/10/49.**C/L.**
Str. 21/10—25/11/50.**G.**
Str. 4/6—24/7/54.**G.**
Str. 27/12/57—27/1/58.**G.**
Str. 5/4—13/5/60.**C/L.**

BOILERS:
2020.
2023 23/7/31.
2035 21/7/33.
2092 11/7/35.
2046 19/3/37.
2016 9/2/39.
2005 26/12/40.
2084 20/11/43.
1974 3/4/46.
1937 2/7/48.
29013 25/11/50.
29113 24/7/54.
29033 27/1/58.

SHEDS:
Gorton.
Stratford 19/11/26.
Ipswich 1/9/33.
Stratford 10/10/33.

RENUMBERED:
9647 3/11/46.
69647 26/6/48.

CONDEMNED: 24/11/60.
Cut up at Stratford.

_____

867

Gorton.

To traffic 19/11/26.

REPAIRS:
Str. 5/10/28—25/1/29.**G.**
Additional coal rails.
Str. 27/12/30—20/2/31.**G.**
Str. 1/10—25/11/32.**G.**
Str. 13/11/34—2/1/35.**G.**
Str. 23/10—1/12/36.**G.**
Condensing gear removed.
Str. 25/8—7/10/38.**G.**
Str. 26/8—23/10/40.**G.**
Str. 15/2—8/3/41.**L.**
Str. 19/3—24/5/43.**G.**
Altered to N7/5.
Str. 22/6—5/8/44.**G.**
Str. 10/6—21/7/45.**G.**
Str. 25/1—15/2/46.**L.**
Str. 22/8—22/9/46.**L.**
Str. 8/4—26/5/48.**G.**
Str. 16/1—24/2/50.**C/L.**
Str. 16/2—17/3/51.**G.**
Str. 19/8—19/9/53.**G.**
Str. 26/8—29/9/56.**G.**
Str. 12/8/60. *Not repaired.*

BOILERS:
2021.
2012 25/11/32.
2102 2/1/35.
2012 1/12/36.
2087 7/10/38.

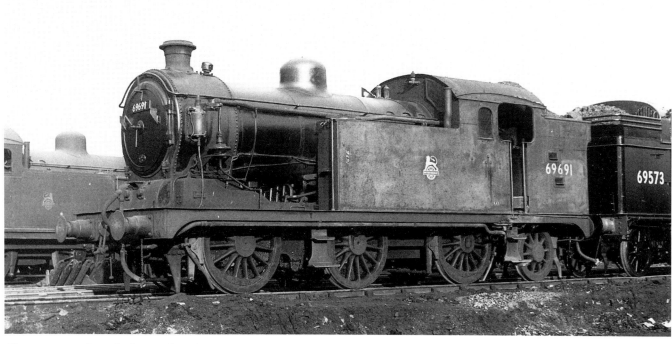

Change to round top firebox on Part 2 began with No.2659, ex-works 10th December 1943 and continued to 8th January 1955 when No.69690 (ex 2650) was altered, all except two being done.

The two Part 2 to retain Belpaire firebox to withdrawal were Nos.69689 (ex 2649) and 69695 (ex 2655) withdrawn on 25th March 1957 and 1st December 1958 respectively. No.69695's boiler started work 7th November 1925 on No.940.

The Part 2 engines rebuilt with round top firebox were then basically the same as Part 3 except in lubrication because they kept the sight feed type.

The thirty-two Part 3 engines had, and retained the Wakefield mechanical type lubricator.

The round-top boilers built from 1935 were to Diagram 101 and had hand holes and inspection covers instead of washout plugs, but in the same positions, three on the left hand side and two on the right hand side.

867 cont./
   982 23/10/40.
2068 24/5/43.
2083 21/7/45.
1959 26/5/48.
29024 17/3/51.
29109 19/9/53.
24802 *(new)* 29/9/56.

SHEDS:
Gorton.
Stratford 3/12/26.
Hatfield 14/9/52.

RENUMBERED:
9648 13/10/46.
69648 22/5/48.

CONDEMNED: 29/8/60.
Cut up at Stratford.

_____

868

Gorton.

To traffic 10/12/26.

REPAIRS:
Str. 12/10/28—31/1/29.**G.**
Additional coal rails.
Str. 30/5—29/7/31.**G.**
Str. 17/10—30/11/32.**L.**
Str. 2/10—31/10/33.**G.**
Str. 4—30/7/35.**G.**
Str. 5/3—13/4/37.**G.**
Condensing gear removed.
Str. 13/1—6/3/39.**G.**
Str. 26/1—13/3/41.**G.**
Str. 9—25/9/42.**L.**
Str. 1/1—5/2/44.**G.**
Altered to N7/5.
Str. 10/4—16/5/45.**G.**
Str. 22/10—9/12/47.**G.**
Str. 15/3—10/4/49.**C/L.**
Str. 10/8—2/9/50.**G.**
Str. 13/5—20/6/53.**G.**
Str. 31/8—10/9/54.**C/L.**
Str. 24/2—14/4/56.**G.**
Str. 20/7/59. *Not repaired.*

BOILERS:
 2022.
2087 29/7/31.
2120 31/10/33.
2094 30/7/35.
2017 13/4/37.
2010 6/3/39.
2100 13/3/41.
1979 5/2/44.
1934 16/5/45.

1917 9/12/47.
1969 2/9/50.
29106 20/6/53.
29123 14/4/56.

SHEDS:
Gorton.
Stratford 13/1/27.
Cambridge 1/6/36.
Stratford 5/6/38.
Cambridge (Bishops Stortford)
1/6/38.
Stratford 5/6/38.
Hatfield 22/11/53.

RENUMBERED:
9649 13/10/46.
69649 9/4/49.

CONDEMNED: 27/7/59.
Cut up at Stratford.

_____

870

Gorton.

To traffic 30/12/26.

REPAIRS:
Str. 12/10/28—29/1/29.**G.**
Additional coal rails.
Str. 25/4—20/6/31.**G.**
Str. 26/6—31/7/33.**G.**
Str. 30/5—3/7/35.**G.**
Str. 10/12/36—18/1/37.**G.**
Condensing gear removed.
Str. 22—31/12/37.**L.**
Str. 14/12/38—25/1/39.**G.**
Str. 15/11—14/12/40.**G.**
Str. 27/12/41—22/1/42.**L.**
Str. 29/1—11/3/44.**G.**
Str. 2/6—6/8/46.**G.**
Altered to N7/5.
Str. 31/8—1/10/49.**G.**
Str. 2/12/52—14/1/53.**G.**
Str. 26/7—19/8/54.**C/L.**
Str. 22/1—9/3/56.**G.**

BOILERS:
 2023.
2089 20/6/31.
2099 31/7/33.
2048 3/7/35.
2116 18/1/37.
2051 25/1/39.
 983 14/12/40.
2051 11/3/44.
1907 6/8/46.
1980 1/10/49.
29085 14/1/53.

29070 9/3/56.

SHEDS:
Gorton.
Stratford 13/1/27.
Hatfield 4/4/54.

RENUMBERED:
9650 8/12/46.
69650 1/10/49.

CONDEMNED: 19/5/59.
Cut up at Stratford.

_____

873

Gorton.

To traffic 5/2/27.

REPAIRS:
Str. 22/9—14/12/28.**G.**
Additional coal rails.
Str. 27/9—5/12/30.**G.**
Str. 1/10—21/11/32.**G.**
Str. 8/1—8/2/35.**G.**
Str. 6—28/2/36.**H.**
Str. 5/1—6/2/37.**G.**
Condensing gear removed.
Str. 2/10—18/11/38.**G.**
Str. 26/10—2/12/40.**G.**
Str. 11/7—25/9/43.**G.**
Str. 11/11—5/12/45.**G.**
Altered to N7/5.
Str. 17/8—21/9/48.**G.**
Str. 2—28/2/49.**L.**
Str. 21/4—14/5/49.**C/L.**
Str. 11/9—20/10/51.**G.**
Push-pull gear fitted.
Westinghouse replaced by steam
brake.
Str. 10/10—15/11/52.**C/L.**
Str. 21/7—21/8/54.**G.**
Str. 29/3—111/5/56.**C/L.**
Str. 6/2—9/3/57.**G.**
Str. 27/7—9/9/60.**C/L.**

BOILERS:
 2024.
2030 21/11/32.
2029 8/2/35.
2046 28/2/36.
2038 6/2/37.
2018 18/11/38.
2112 2/12/40.
2011 25/9/43.
1946 5/12/45.
2070 21/9/48.
29041 20/10/51.
29100 21/8/54.

24803 *(new)* 9/3/57.

SHEDS:
Gorton.
Stratford 10/2/27.
Colwick 22/4/51.
Annesley 23/12/51.
Cambridge 30/9/56.
Stratford 17/8/58.
King's Lynn 26/7/59.
Stratford 20/9/59.
Parkeston 24/1/60.
Stratford 24/7/60.
Parkeston 16/10/60.
Stratford 1/1/61.

RENUMBERED:
9651 25/10/46.
69651 18/9/48.

CONDEMNED: 13/1/61.
Cut up at Stratford.

_____

907

R.Stephenson & Co. 3897.

To traffic 2/10/25.

REPAIRS:
Str. 26/5—31/8/28.**G.**
Additional coal rails.
Str. 16/8—24/10/30.**G.**
Str. 19/12/32—27/1/33.**G.**
Str. 23/10—30/11/34.**G.**
Str. 1/12/36—13/1/37.**G.**
Condensing gear removed.
Str. 15/10—29/11/38.**G.**
Str. 29/9—26/11/40.**G.**
Str. 30/5—17/8/43.**G.**
Str. 30/9—27/10/45.**G.**
Altered to N7/5.
Str. 8/1—21/2/48.**G.**
Str. 10/8—16/9/50.**G.**
Str. 5—31/10/53.**G.**
Str. 29/10—24/11/56.**G.**
Str. 30/6—4/7/58.**C/L.**
Str. 30/12/59—19/2/60.**L/I.**
Str. 12/8—3/10/60.**C/L.**

BOILERS:
 2025.
2121 24/10/30.
2093 27/1/33.
2038 30/11/34.
2013 13/1/37.
2100 29/11/38.
2026 26/11/40.
2090 17/8/43.
1942 27/10/45.

_____

WORKS CODES:- Cw - Cowlairs. Dar- Darlington. Don - Doncaster. Ghd - Gateshead. Gor - Gorton. Inv - Inverurie. Str - Stratford.
REPAIR CODES:- **C/H** - Casual Heavy. **C/L** - Casual Light. **G** - General. **H**- Heavy. **H/I** - Heavy Intermediate. **L** - Light. **L/I** - Light Intermediate. **N/C** - Non-Classified.

For possible working over the Metropolitan Railway lines, Nos.457 and 913 (31st December 1926) also No.919 (2nd February 1927), were fitted with trip cock gear, the striker being just to the rear of the cab footstep. All three had the gear removed on 1st April 1931.

Nos.2642 to 2661 arrived from their Glasgow builder with Metropolitan trip cock gear already fitted. Note the striker was located in the same position on both sides of the engine. They too had the gear removed in 1931/2 (*see* page 26, top).

In March 1957 Nos.69625, 69630, 69643, and in November 1957 Nos.69691 and 69696 had trip cock gear fitted for work on the Epping line, and when 69625 was withdrawn on the 17th April 1959 its gear was put on 69708.

Ex-works 5th January 1947, No.9616 was fitted with a 'Jay-Gee' smoke eliminator. Two air inlets were provided on the sides of the smokebox leading to four of the lower boiler tubes to provide additional air in the firebox. This did not prove successful and when 9616 went in for repair on 31st July 1949, this apparatus was removed.

907 cont./
  1924 21/2/48.
29004 16/9/50.
29142 31/10/53.
29109 24/11/56.

SHEDS:
Gorton.
Hatfield 20/10/25.
Stratford 30/11/28.
Colchester 14/10/58.
Stratford 6/12/59.

RENUMBERED:
  9652 3/11/46.
E9652 21/2/48.
69652 16/9/50.

CONDEMNED: 4/12/60.
Cut up at Stratford.

_____

912

R.Stephenson & Co. 3898.

To traffic 7/10/25.

REPAIRS:
Str. 17/10/27—6/1/28.**G**.
Additional coal rails.
Str. 30/11/29—7/2/30.**G**.
Str. 19/12/31—13/2/32.**G**.
Str. 17/10—25/11/32.**L**.
Str. 22/2—29/3/34.**G**.
Str. 21/11—17/12/35.**G**.
Str. 19/7—25/8/37.**G**.
Condensing gear removed.
Str. 11/4—20/5/39.**G**.
Str. 11/5—17/6/41.**G**.
Str. 7/5—9/6/44.**G**.
Str. 29/9—1/11/46.**G**.
Don. 16/4—15/7/48.**L**.
Str. 8/7—3/9/49.**G**.
Str. 22/7—3/9/52.**G**.
Altered to N7/5.
Str. 16/12/54—21/1/55.**C/L**.
Str. 26/6—1/9/56.**G**.
Str. 14/9—30/10/59.**G**.

BOILERS:
  2026.
  2106 13/2/32.
  2096 29/3/34.
  2011 17/12/35.
  2120 25/8/37.
  2024 20/5/39.
  2054 17/6/41.
  2017 9/6/44.
  2114 1/11/46.
  2112 3/9/49.
29075 3/9/52.
29084 1/9/56.
29021 30/10/59.

SHEDS:
Ardsley.
King's Cross 3/11/25.
Stratford 15/10/27.

RENUMBERED:
  9653 16/11/46.
69653 15/7/48.

CONDEMNED: 3/5/62.
Cut up at Stratford.

_____

913

R.Stephenson & Co. 3899.

To traffic 12/10/25.

REPAIRS:
Trip cock fitted 31/12/26.
Str. 11/2—2/5/28.**G**.
Additional coal rails.
Str. 9/11/30—9/1/31.**G**.
Trip cock removed 1/4/31.
Str. 2/3—10/4/33.**G**.
Str. 15/2—28/3/35.**G**.
Str. 10/1—20/2/37.**G**.
Condensing gear removed.
Str. 14/9—25/10/38.**G**.
Str. 5/7—16/8/40.**G**.
Str. 29/1—22/3/43.**G**.
Str. 13/5—15/6/45.**G**.
Str. 14/12/47—21/2/48.**G**.
Str. 8/3—12/4/51.**G**.
Altered to N7/5.
Str. 19/7—27/8/55.**G**.
Str. 29/4—15/6/58.**G**.
Str. 7—18/9/59.**C/L**.

BOILERS:
  2027.
  989 9/1/31.
2121 10/4/33.
2009 28/3/35.
2041 20/2/37.
2036 25/10/38.
  980 16/8/40.
2032 22/3/43.
2035 15/6/45.
2052 21/2/48.
29026 12/4/51.
29138 *(new)* 27/8/55.
29045 15/6/58.

SHEDS:
Ardsley.
Hatfield 3/11/25.
King's Cross 10/3/28.
Hatfield 6/5/28.
King's Cross 29/7/28.
Stratford 9/1/31.
Colwick 6/7/52.
Hatfield 11/4/54.
Stratford 31/1/60.

RENUMBERED:
  9654 22/11/46.
E9654 21/2/48.
69654 12/4/51.

CONDEMNED: 4/12/60.
Cut up at Stratford.

_____

916

R.Stephenson & Co. 3900.

To traffic 14/10/25.

REPAIRS:
Str. 9/5—21/8/28.**G**.
Additional coal rails.
Str. 14/6—29/8/30.**G**.
Str. 9/7—6/9/32.**G**.
Str. 12/7—23/8/34.**G**.
Str. 16/6—22/7/36.**G**.
Condensing gear removed.
Str. 27/10—7/12/37.**G**.
Str. 25/11/39—4/1/40.**G**.
Str. 23/10—6/11/41.**L**.
Str. 23/5—1/7/42.**G**.
Str. 4/2—10/3/45.**G**.
Str. 26/10—2/12/46.**G**.
Str. 27/6—13/8/49.**G**.
Str. 2/1—14/2/53.**G**.
Altered to N7/5.
Str. 8—28/2/56.**C/L**.
Str. 1/10—9/11/56.**G**.
Str. 7/8/59. *Not repaired.*

BOILERS:
  2028.
  2041 6/9/32.
  2042 23/8/34.
  987 22/7/36.
2105 7/12/37.
2033 4/1/40.
2031 1/7/42.
2050 2/12/46.
2119 13/8/49.
29090 14/2/53.
29075 9/11/56.

SHEDS:
Ardsley.
King's Cross 9/11/25.
Stratford 24/1/29.

RENUMBERED:
  9655 16/11/46.
69655 13/8/49.

CONDEMNED: 10/8/59.
Cut up at Stratford.

_____

918

R.Stephenson & Co. 3901.

To traffic 24/10/25.

REPAIRS:
Str. 25/11/27—23/2/28.**G**.
Additional coal rails.
Str. 1/2—21/3/30.**G**.
Str. 12/3—15/4/32.**G**.
Str. 9—25/4/34.**G**.
Str. 5/2—2/3/36.**G**.
Str. 30/4—29/5/37.**L**.
Str. 8/1—16/2/38.**G**.
Condensing gear removed.
Str. 7/12/39—25/1/40.**G**.
Str. 22/5—26/6/42.**G**.
Str. 6/10—9/11/44.**G**.
Str. 8—20/4/45.**L**.
Str. 24/11/47—10/1/48.**G**.
Altered to N7/5.
Str. 1/9—7/10/50.**G**.
Str. 13/7—29/8/53.**G**.
Str. 29/8—20/9/56.**C/L**.
Str. 10—20/12/56.**C/L**.
Str. 20/9—1/11/57.**G**.
Str. 20/1—5/2/60.**N/C**.
Str. 25/8—3/9/60.**C/L**.

BOILERS:
  2029.
  2042 15/4/32.
  2026 25/4/34.
  2096 2/3/36.
  2097 16/2/38.
  986 25/1/40.
2120 26/6/42.
2093 9/11/44.
1921 10/1/48.
29002 7/10/50.
29030 29/8/53.
29097 1/11/57.

SHEDS:
Gorton.
Neasden 10/11/25.
Stratford 27/9/26.

RENUMBERED:
  9656 18/10/46.
69656 7/10/50.

CONDEMNED: 10/4/61.
Cut up at Stratford.

_____

Nos.69633 and 69634 were fitted with a small steam stop valve to the rear of the dome so that they could operate a pump during the night at their Buntingford stabling point (there was no 'shed') to raise water from a nearby well into the depot supply tank.

For use on the M&GN line from Melton Constable to and from Cromer and Sheringham, Nos.69708 (22nd) and 69679 (28th) were equipped with Whittaker tablet exchanging apparatus in September 1948.

The tablet apparatus was fitted on both sides and recessed into the cab side sheets. Both had the apparatus removed when they left the M&GN section on 1st February 1959. Note addition of push and pull gear at May 1957 repair.

During June-August 1949 Nos.69689, 69690, 69692, 69694 and 69698 were fitted with vacuum controlled regulator for push and pull working out of Marylebone. The control gear was on the left hand side of the smokebox and a large anti-vacuum valve was added on the right hand side.

919

R.Stephenson & Co. 3902.

To traffic 29/10/25.

REPAIRS:
Trip cock gear fitted 2/2/27.
Str. 11/2—28/4/28.**G**.
Additional coal rails.
Str. 11/7—26/9/30.**G**.
Trip cock gear removed 1/4/31.
Str. 1/9—19/10/32.**G**.
Str. 23/12/34—5/2/35.**G**.
Str. 4—30/10/36.**G**.
Condensing gear removed.
Str. 6—24/3/38.**L**.
Str. 10/7—15/8/38.**G**.
Str. 23/6—3/8/40.**G**.
Str. 14—24/1/41.**L**.
Str. 4/8—26/9/42.**H**.
Str. 7/1—17/2/45.**G**.
Str. 10/1—19/3/48.**G**.
Str. 9—24/12/48.**C/L**.
Str. 4/8—3/9/49.**C/L**.
Str. 26/11/50—6/1/51.**G**.
Altered to N7/5.
Str. 30/9—31/10/53.**G**.
Str. 6/12/55—10/2/56.**C/H**.
Str. 1/2—9/3/57.**G**.
Str. 2/6/59. *Not repaired.*

BOILERS:
 2030.
 2048 19/10/32.
 2037 5/2/35.
 2051 30/10/36.
 2104 15/8/38.
 2020 3/8/40.
 2007 26/9/42.
 2102 17/2/45.
 2046 19/3/48.
29014 6/1/51.
29024 31/10/53.
29036 9/3/57.

SHEDS:
Gorton.
Hatfield 6/11/25.
King's Cross 10/3/28.
Hatfield 6/5/28.
King's Cross 6/9/28.
Stratford 26/9/30.

RENUMBERED:
 9657 22/8/46.
ᴇ9657 19/3/48.
69657 24/12/48.

CONDEMNED: 8/6/59.
Cut up at Straford.

935

R.Stephenson & Co. 3903.

To traffic 3/11/25.

REPAIRS:
Str. 12/8—28/10/27.**G**.
Additional coal rails.
Str. 27/9—16/11/29.**G**.
Str. 5/9—20/11/31.**G**.
Str. 5/6—19/7/34.**G**.
Str. 29/4—9/6/36.**G**.
Condensing gear removed.
Str. 1/2—11/3/38.**G**.
Str. 7/4—23/5/40.**G**.
Str. 7/11/42—5/1/43.**G**.
Str. 20/5—16/6/45.**G**.
Str. 7/12/47—24/1/48.**G**.
Str. 14/7—24/8/50.**G**.
Altered to N7/5.
Str. 9/12/52—17/1/53.**G**.
Str. 15/11—3/12/54.**C/L**.
Str. 17/12/54—29/1/55.**C/L**.
Str. 19/9—5/11/55.**G**.
Str. 13/9—27/10/56.**C/L**.
Str. 30/1—16/2/57.**C/L**.
Str. 17/2—29/3/58.**G**.
Str. 8/2—14/4/60.**C/L**.

BOILERS:
 2031.
  988 20/11/31.
 2119 19/7/34.
 2049 9/6/36.
 2096 11/3/38.
 2027 23/5/40.
 2048 5/1/43.
 2095 16/6/45.
 2105 24/1/48.
 1995 24/8/50.
29121 17/1/53.
29001 5/11/55.
29096 29/3/58.

SHEDS:
Gorton.
Neasden 10/11/25.
Stratford 27/9/26.

RENUMBERED:
 9658 12/10/46.
ᴇ9658 24/1/48.
69658 24/8/50.

CONDEMNED: 7/4/61.
Cut up at Stratford.

940

R.Stephenson & Co. 3904.

To traffic 7/11/25.

REPAIRS:
Str. 24/3—30/6/28.**G**.
Additional coal rails.
Str. 9/8—17/10/30.**G**.
Str. 18/10—25/11/32.**G**.
Str. 11/10—26/11/34.**G**.
Str. 22/10—8/11/35.**L**.
Str. 9/9—14/10/36.**G**.
Cond gear removed.
Str. 19/6—16/7/38.**G**.
Str. 17/6—19/7/40.**G**.
Str. 14/4—11/6/43.**G**.
Str. 24/6—2/8/45.**G**.
Str. 25/1—25/3/48.**G**.
Str. 1/10—8/11/50.**G**.
Altered to N7/5.
Str. 12/2—18/3/53.**G**.
Str. 2/1—11/2/56.**G**.
Str. 7/10/57—20/1/58.**C/L**.

BOILERS:
 2032.
 2015 17/10/30.
 2044 25/11/32.
 2010 26/11/34.
 2008 14/10/36.
 2042 16/7/38.
 2106 19/7/40.
 2027 11/6/43.
 2049 2/8/45.
 2096 25/3/48.
29010 8/11/50.
29007 18/3/53.
29068 11/2/56.

SHEDS:
Gorton.
Neasden 30/11/25.
Stratford 27/9/26.

RENUMBERED:
 9659 25/8/46.
69659 25/3/48.

CONDEMNED: 19/1/59.
Cut up at Stratford.

941

R.Stephenson & Co. 3905.

To traffic 14/11/25.

REPAIRS:
Str. 7/4—7/7/28.**G**.
Additional coal rails.
Str. 10/5—18/7/30.**G**.
Str. 4/7—20/8/32.**G**.
Str. 31/7—3/10/34.**G**.
Str. 6/8—4/9/36.**G**.
Condensing gear removed.
Str. 15/10—23/11/38.**G**.
Str. 25/9—7/12/40.**G**.
Str. 3—18/10/41.**L**.
Str. 24/7—24/9/43.**G**.
Altered to N7/5.
Str. 5—25/11/44.**G**.
Str. 14/10—9/11/45.**G**.
Str. 6/7—9/9/48.**G**.
Str. 8/4—11/5/51.**G**.
Str. 21/4—10/5/52.**C/L**.
Str. 12/1—12/2/53.**C/L**.
Str. 21/4—22/5/53.**C/L**.
Str. 4—30/1/54.**G**.
Str. 29/7—15/9/54.**C/L**.
Str. 22/9—26/10/55.**C/L**.
Str. 11/10—17/11/56.**G**.

BOILERS:
 2033.
  982 20/8/32.
 2040 3/10/34.
 2016 4/9/36.
 2005 23/11/38.
 2087 7/12/40.
 1971 24/9/43.
 1972 9/11/45.
 1974 9/9/48.
29028 11/5/51.
29103 30/1/54.
29003 17/11/56.

SHEDS:
Ardsley.
Neasden 30/11/25.
Stratford 27/9/26.

RENUMBERED:
 9660 19/8/46.
69660 9/9/48.

CONDEMNED: 18/5/59.
Cut up at Stratford.

947

R.Stephenson & Co. 3906.

To traffic 18/11/25.

REPAIRS:
Str. 18/11/27—3/2/28.**G.**
Additional coal rails.
Str. 28/6—12/9/30.**G.**
Str. 30/9—2/11/32.**G.**
Str. 24/7—20/9/34.**G.**
Str. 28/8—8/10/36.**G.**
Condensing gear removed.
Str. 21/6—18/7/38.**G.**
Str. 21/4—24/5/40.**G.**
Str. 21/11/42—1/1/43.**G.**
Str. 15/4—5/5/45.**G.**
Str. 7/3—15/5/48.**G.**
Str. 3/12/50—6/1/51.**G.**
Altered to N7/5.
Str. 29/7—12/9/53.**G.**
Str. 22—25/9/53.**N/C.**
Str. 23/5—18/8/56.**G.**
Str. 18—28/6/57.**C/L.**
Str. 13/1—19/2/58.**C/L.**
Str. 16/10/59. *Not repaired.*

BOILERS:
2034.
2054 2/11/32.
2100 20/9/34.
988 8/10/36.
2119 18/7/38.
981 24/5/40.
2019 1/1/43.
2097 5/5/45.
2035 15/5/48.
29109 6/1/51.
29094 12/9/53.
29091 18/8/56.

SHEDS:
Ardsley.
Stratford 22/12/25.

RENUMBERED:
9661 17/8/46.
69661 15/5/48.

CONDEMNED: 19/10/59.
Cut up at Stratford.

_____

950

R.Stephenson & Co. 3907.

To traffic 23/11/25.

REPAIRS:
Str. 11/11/27—8/2/28.**G.**
Additional coal rails.
Str. 14/6—22/8/30.**G.**
Str. 13/9—18/10/32.**G.**

Str. 7/6—27/7/34.**G.**
Str. 16/2—19/3/36.**G.**
Str. 31/12/37—28/1/38.**G.**
Condensing gear removed.
Str. 12/11—21/12/39.**G.**
Str. 18/4—29/5/42.**G.**
Str. 31/12/44—26/1/45.**G.**
Str. 16/5—26/6/47.**G.**
Str. 29/12/49—4/2/50.**G.**
Str. 21/8—27/9/52.**G.**
Str. 10/1—12/2/55.**G.**
Altered to N7/5.
Str. 16/2—20/3/56.**C/L.**
Str. 16/7—20/8/57.**G.**

BOILERS:
2035.
2114 18/10/32.
2112 19/3/36.
2021 28/1/38.
2052 21/12/39.
2015 29/5/42.
2101 26/1/45.
2113 26/6/47.
27860 27/9/52.
29133 *(new)* 12/2/55.
29029 20/8/57.

SHEDS:
Gorton.
Stratford 9/12/25.

RENUMBERED:
9662 24/8/46.
69662 4/2/50.

CONDEMNED: 4/5/59.
Cut up at Stratford.

_____

952

R.Stephenson & Co. 3908.

To traffic 2/12/25.

REPAIRS:
Str. 13/1—4/4/28.**G.**
Additional coal rails.
Str. 22/3—16/5/30.**G.**
Str. 9/4—31/5/32.**G.**
Str. 24/8—30/10/34.**G.**
Str. 30/10—11/12/36.**G.**
Condensing gear removed.
Str. 30/8—15/9/37.**L.**
Str. 4/12/38—11/1/39.**G.**
Str. 1/12/40—31/1/41.**G.**
Str. 5/12/43—8/1/44.**G.**
Str. 19/5—22/7/46.**G.**
Altered to N7/5.
Str. 31/3—14/5/49.**G.**
Str. 10/4—12/5/51.**G.**
Str. 22/3—1/4/53.**C/L.**
Str. 11/5—12/6/53.**G.**
Str. 7/11—23/12/55.**G.**

Str. 10/3—24/5/58.**G.**
Str. 4—21/5/59.**C/L.**
Str. 7/1—4/3/60.**C/L.**

BOILERS:
2036.
2038 31/5/32.
2053 30/10/34.
2037 11/12/36.
2054 11/1/39.
2008 31/1/41.
2118 8/1/44.
1905 22/7/46.
1954 14/5/49.
29030 12/5/51.
29101 12/6/53.
24800 *(new)* 23/12/55.
29081 24/5/58.

SHEDS:
Ardsley.
Stratford 18/12/25.

RENUMBERED:
9663 14/10/46.
69663 14/5/49.

CONDEMNED: 1/11/60.
Cut up at Stratford.

_____

964

R. Stephenson & Co. 3909.

To traffic 7/12/25.

REPAIRS:
Str. 9/12/27—14/3/28.**G.**
Additional coal rails.
Str. 19/4—18/6/30.**G.**
Str. 12/3—27/4/32.**G.**
Str. 8/2—22/3/34.**G.**
Str. 29/11/35—2/1/36.**G.**
Str. 26/7—1/9/37.**G.**
Condensing gear removed.
Str. 11/6—29/7/39.**G.**
Str. 15—26/2/41.**L.**
Str. 17/11—20/12/41.**G.**
Str. 25/11/43—8/1/44.**G.**
Altered to N7/5.
Str. 21/9—17/11/45.**G.**
Str. 28/4—29/5/47.**L.**
Str. 16/7—12/9/47.**L.**
Str. 13/6—13/8/48.**G.**
Str. 11/5—29/6/51.**G.**
Str. 13—25/8/53.**C/L.**
Str. 10/5—25/6/54.**G.**
Str. 18—27/4/56.**C/L.**
Str. 27/9—27/10/56.**G.**
Str. 28/5—19/6/58.**C/L.**
Str. 4/2—11/3/60.**C/L.**
Str. 7—23/9/60.**C/L.**

BOILERS:
2037.
2049 27/4/32.
2020 22/3/34.
2095 2/1/36.
2053 1/9/37.
2093 29/7/39.
2047 20/12/41.
1978 8/1/44.
1944 17/11/45.
1966 13/8/48.
29032 29/6/51.
29031 25/6/54.
29004 27/10/56.

SHEDS:
Gorton.
Stratford 18/12/25.

RENUMBERED:
9664 14/10/46.
69664 13/8/48.

CONDEMNED: 30/11/60.
Cut up at Stratford.

_____

966

R. Stephenson & Co. 3910.

To traffic 11/12/25.

REPAIRS:
Str. 5—27/3/26.**L.**
Str. 2/12/27—10/3/28.**G.**
Additional coal rails.
Str. 13/12/29—20/2/30.**G.**
Str. 20/2—15/4/32.**G.**
Str. 27/1—6/3/34.**G.**
Str. 6/12/35—10/1/36.**G.**
Str. 25/10—23/11/37.**G.**
Condensing gear removed.
Str. 7/9—13/10/39.**G.**
Str. 6/12/41—13/1/42.**G.**
Str. 21/5—15/7/44.**G.**
Str. 7/11—13/12/46.**G.**
Str. 26/6—20/8/49.**G.**
Str. 19/6—28/7/50.**C/L.**
Str. 22/5—2/7/52.**G.**
Altered to N7/5.
Str. 5—21/11/53.**C/L.**
Str. 20/1—5/3/55.**G.**
Str. 4/5—25/7/56.**C/L.**
Str. 15/11—1/12/56.**C/L.**
Str. 17/7—22/8/57.**G.**
Str. 9/2/60. *Not repaired.*

BOILERS:
2038.
2046 15/4/32.
2027 6/3/34.
989 10/1/36.
2099 23/11/37.
2030 13/10/39.

Between September and November 1951 four more, Nos.69651, 69691, 69695 and 69696 were fitted for push and pull working in the Nottingham area and at Hatfield. They had an improved control system with a second vacuum cylinder on the right hand side of the smokebox. 69651 had to be converted from Westinghouse to steam brake as had 69708 in January 1954 when it had P&P gear fitted.

Only the twenty built by Beardmore, Nos.2642 to 2661, did not originally have Westinghouse brake (*see* page 46, bottom). In June 1933 Nos.2653, 2657, 2660 and 2661, followed by 2659 in September 1933 were sent from GN to GE Section and were changed from steam and vacuum brake to Westinghouse and vacuum. Seven more, Nos.2642 to 2648 had the same treatment in 1938-40. Nos.2649 to 2652 and 2654, 2655, 2656 and 2658 never had Westinghouse and all eight were later fitted for push and pull working.

From 1956 No.69614 was officially designated as 'West Side Pilot' at Liverpool Street station and in October was given special painting. Its crews were then given a special allowance because they had to clean it every day.

The first of the 1921 batch was given the same painting as the two built in 1915, and only these three carried GER. All were painted unlined grey and had a large brass numberplate on the bunker.

Nos.1003 to 1011 were also in unlined grey with a large number plate, but instead of company initials had the number on the tank sides in 19in. high yellow painted and unshaded figures.

Nos.1000 and 1002 to 1011 remained in grey after their first LNER repair. None got the new company initials in any form, and their painted number did not get area suffix E which would have been applicable to Nos.1000 and 1006, 1009, 1010 and 1011, ex-works from 1st September to 29th December 1923. The only change on these eleven was the substitution of a small LNER number plate on the bunker for the large GER brass plate - a clearly visible alteration.

966 cont./
2053 13/1/42.
2112 13/12/46.
2118 20/8/49.
29072 2/7/52.
29047 5/3/55.
29028 22/8/57.

SHEDS:
Gorton.
Stratford 18/12/25.

RENUMBERED:
9665 25/8/46.
69665 20/8/49.

CONDEMNED: 29/2/60.
Cut up at Stratford.

967

R. Stephenson & Co. 3911.

To traffic 15/12/25.

REPAIRS:
Str. 21/10/27—6/1/28.**G**.
Additional coal rails.
Str. 28/3—23/5/30.**G**.
Str. 19/4—30/5/32.**G**.
Str. 2/3—12/4/34.**G**.
Str. 9/1—6/2/36.**G**.
Str. 13/6—3/7/37.**L**.
Str. 16/9—14/10/37.**G**.
Condensing gear removed.
Str. 30/8—10/10/39.**G**.
Str. 22/2—17/4/42.**G**.
Str. 10/12/44—18/1/45.**G**.
Altered to N7/5.
Str. 23/11—24/12/47.**G**.
Str. 16/8—4/9/48.**L**.
Str. 2/11—2/12/50.**G**.
Str. 23/5—12/6/52.**C/L**.
Str. 3/6—3/7/53.**G**.
Str. 3/7—8/9/56.**G**.
Str. 17—18/9/56.**N/C**.
Str. 28/9—3/10/56.**N/C**.
Str. 26/2/59. *Not repaired.*

BOILERS:
2039.
983 30/5/32.
2021 12/4/34.
2099 6/2/36.
2121 14/10/37.
2092 10/10/39.
2117 17/4/42.
1959 18/1/45.
1920 24/12/47.
29105 2/12/50.
29018 3/7/53.
29020 8/9/56.

SHEDS:
Gorton.
Stratford 29/12/25.

RENUMBERED:
9666 25/8/46.
69666 4/9/48.

CONDEMNED: 9/3/59.
Cut up at Stratford.

968

R. Stephenson & Co. 3912.

To traffic 21/12/25.

REPAIRS:
Str. ?/?—25/8/26.**L**.
Fitted with special bunker
Str. 9/12/27—29/2/28.**G**.
Str. 8/2—29/3/30.**G**.
Str. 4/1—20/2/32.**G**.
Str. 21/12/33—25/1/34.**G**.
Special bunker removed.
Additional coal rails fitted.
Str. 8/10—4/11/35.**G**.
Str. 7—21/8/36.**L**.
Str. 29/8—28/9/37.**G**.
Condensing gear removed.
Str. 7/7—24/8/39.**G**.
Str. 22/2—1/5/42.**G**.
Additional washout plugs.
Str. 11/3—18/4/45.**G**.
Str. 9/11—5/12/45.**L**.
Str. 11/12/46—18/1/47.**G**.
Str. 22/7—17/9/49.**G**.
Altered to N7/5.
Str. 3/5—19/6/52.**G**.
Str. 1—27/11/54.**G**.
Str. 26/3—8/5/57.**G**.
Str. 3—22/10/58.**C/L**.

BOILERS:
2040.
2113 20/2/32.
2087 25/1/34.
2034 4/11/35.
2011 28/9/37.
2031 24/8/39.
2097 1/5/42.
2116 18/4/45.
2031 18/1/47.
1963 17/9/49.
29115 *(new)* 19/6/52.
29028 27/11/54.
29054 8/5/57.

SHEDS:
Ardsley.
Stratford 7/1/26.

RENUMBERED:
9667 15/11/46.
69667 17/9/49.

CONDEMNED: 3/2/59.
Cut up at Stratford.

970

R. Stephenson & Co. 3913.

To traffic 24/12/25.

REPAIRS:
Str. 4/11/27—15/2/28.**G**.
Additional coal rails.
Str. 11/4—30/5/30.**G**.
Str. 19/4—3/6/32.**G**.
Str. 16/6—25/7/34.**G**.
Str. 5/4—19/5/36.**G**.
Condensing gear removed.
Str. 7/12/37—7/1/38.**G**.
Str. 3/12/39—13/1/40.**G**.
Str. 29/5—23/7/42.**G**.
Str. 20/12/44—10/2/45.**G**.
Str. 7/12/47—18/2/48.**G**.
Str. 17/9—21/10/50.**G**.
Altered to N7/5.
Str. 24/3—1/5/53.**G**.
Str. 29/7—25/8/54.**C/L**.
Str. 26/7—13/10/55.**G**.
Str. 4/11—14/12/57.**G**.
Str. 29/1—26/2/60.**C/L**.
Str. 2/1—7/2/61.**N/C**.

BOILERS:
2041.
987 3/6/32.
2104 25/7/34.
2022 19/5/36.
987 7/1/38.
2009 13/1/40.
2022 23/7/42.
2043 18/2/48.
29102 21/10/50.
29092 1/5/53.
29051 13/10/55.
29059 14/12/57.

SHEDS:
Ardsley.
Stratford 20/1/26.

RENUMBERED:
9668 21/12/46.
ᴇ**9668** 18/2/48.
69668 21/10/50.

CONDEMNED: 10/9/61.
Cut up at Stratford.

971

R. Stephenson & Co. 3914.

To traffic 4/1/26.

REPAIRS:
Str. 31/12/27—30/3/28.**G**.
Additional coal rails.
Str. 20/12/29—14/2/30.**G**.
Str. 2/1—18/3/32.**G**.
Str. 19/4—25/5/34.**G**.
Str. 20/1—27/2/36.**G**.
Str. 15/12/37—22/1/38.**G**.
Condensing gear removed.
Str. 28—31/1/38.**N/C**.
Str. 24/10—2/12/39.**G**.
Str. 18/4—5/6/42.**G**.
Str. 11/2—17/3/45.**G**.
Str. 11/8—24/9/47.**G**.
Altered to N7/5.
Str. 12/1—9/2/48.**L**.
Str. 9/2—6/4/50.**G**.
Str. 13—29/9/51.**C/L**.
Str. 9/3—16/4/53.**G**.
Str. 28/5—23/6/53.**C/L**.
Str. 30/6—27/8/55.**G**.
Str. 23/10—23/11/57.**G**.

BOILERS:
2042.
2016 18/3/32.
2022 25/5/34.
2027 27/2/36.
2032 22/1/38.
984 2/12/39.
2039 5/6/42.
2077 24/9/47.
2077 reno.29044 29/9/51.
29125 *(new)* 16/4/53.
29076 27/8/55.
29111 23/11/57.

SHEDS:
Gorton.
Stratford 22/1/26.

RENUMBERED:
9669 16/10/46
69669 6/4/50

CONDEMNED: 6/4/59.
Cut up at Stratford.

987

R. Stephenson & Co. 3915.

To traffic 9/1/26.

REPAIRS:
Str. 23/12/27—30/3/28.**G**.
Additional coal rails.
Str. 3/5—16/7/30.**G**.

(*above*) No.1001 was out from a general repair in February 1922 when 19in. figures replaced GER initials. When next ex-works on 9th May 1924 it was as 8001 but still on unlined grey and with the bunker number plate changed as on the other eleven. It was the only N7 to carry 1924 numbering on grey.

(*left*) Nos.990 to 999 all had the area suffix E when they were new despite the last three being ex-works after it had been discarded. They had standard LNER black livery and single red lining and included 4½in. shaded letter and numbers on the buffer beams.

Whilst the fifty Part 1 engines had standard black paint and lining, curiously the twenty built by R. Stephenson & Co. arrived with pure GER style 6in. serif letter and figures on the buffer beams – 2³/₄ years after these had lost currency.

987 cont./
Str. 7/5—8/7/32.**G.**
Str. 9/8—8/10/34.**G.**
Str. 19/7—24/8/36.**G.**
Condensing gear removed.
Str. 25/5—24/6/37.**L.**
Str. 15/5—17/6/38.**G.**
Str. 13—22/12/38.**L.**
Str. 31/3—11/5/40.**G.**
Str. 10—31/7/41.**L.**
Str. 6/9—3/10/42.**G.**
Str. 18/1—23/2/45.**G.**
Str. 2/11—16/12/47.**G.**
Str. 31/8—16/9/49.**C/L.**
Str. 23/9—1/11/50.**G.**
Altered to N7/5.
Str. 28/6—2/7/52.**C/L.**
Str. 3/3—10/4/53.**G.**
Str. 22/8—7/10/55.**G.**
Str. 12/11—21/12/57.**G.**
Str. 29/3—29/4/60.**C/L.**

BOILERS:
2043.
2047 8/7/32.
988 8/10/34.
2104 24/8/36.
2106 17/6/38.
2095 11/5/40.
2052 3/10/42.
2098 16/12/47.
29104 1/11/50.
29017 10/4/53.
29000 7/10/55.
29137 21/12/57.

SHEDS:
Gorton.
Stratford 22/1/26.

RENUMBERED:
9670 15/12/46.
69670 1/11/50.

CONDEMNED: 10/9/61.
Cut up at Stratford.

988

R. Stephenson & Co. 3916.

To traffic 16/1/26.

REPAIRS:
Str. 31/12/27—10/3/28.**G.**
Additional coal rails.
Str. 17/5—30/7/30.**G.**
Str. 6/9—5/10/32.**G.**
Str. 19/7—24/8/34.**G.**
Str. 8/6—15/7/36.**G.**
Condensing gear removed.
Str. 18/3—21/4/38.**G.**
Str. 16/1—24/2/40.**G.**
Str. 1/3—17/4/42.**G.**

Str. 15/10—30/11/44.**G.**
Str. 26/8—22/10/47.**G.**
Str. 25/11/49—2/1/50.**G.**
Altered to N7/5.
Str. 21/7—29/8/52.**G.**
Str. 12—23/4/54.**C/L.**
Str. 2/11—4/12/54.**G.**
Str. 24/9—13/10/56.**C/L.**
Str. 7/3—12/4/57.**G.**
Str. 20/10—24/12/59.**G.**

BOILERS:
2044.
2051 5/10/32.
2016 24/8/34.
985 15/7/36.
982 21/4/38.
2021 24/2/40.
2094 17/4/42.
2092 30/11/44.
2021 22/10/47.
1914 2/1/50.
29119 *(new)* 29/8/52.
29029 4/12/54.
29086 12/4/57.
29084 24/12/59.

SHEDS:
Gorton.
Stratford 4/2/26.

RENUMBERED:
9671 24/8/46.
69671 2/1/50.

CONDEMNED: 16/9/62.
Cut up at Stratford.

2632

Gorton.

To traffic 3/11/27.

REPAIRS:
Str. 15/2—5/4/30.**G.**
Str. 28/11/31—22/1/32.**G.**
Str. 5/7—24/8/34.**G.**
Str. 21/6—24/7/36.**G.**
Condensing gear removed.
Str. 12/8—23/9/38.**G.**
Str. 8/10—2/12/40.**G.**
Str. 1/3—3/4/42.**L.**
Str. 22/5—13/8/43.**G.**
Str. 8/7—11/8/45.**G.**
Str. 27/8—29/10/47.**G.**
Str. 17/8—30/9/50.**G.**
Str. 9—17/10/50.**N/C.**
Altered to N7/3.
Str. 13—22/3/52.**C/L.**
Str. 13/4—15/5/53.**G.**
Str. 6/6—3/8/56.**G.**

BOILERS:
2045.
2101 22/1/32.
2018 24/7/36.
2008 23/9/38.
2050 2/12/40.
982 13/8/43.
2027 11/8/45.
2039 29/10/47.
29101 30/9/50.
29010 15/5/53.
24801 *(new)* 3/8/56.

SHEDS:
Gorton.
Hatfield 8/12/27.
Stratford 18/1/29.
Lincoln 29/5/49.
Stratford 23/4/50.
Colchester 11/11/51.
Stratford 22/9/52.
Colchester 26/10/52.
Stratford 4/3/56.
Parkeston 28/10/56.

RENUMBERED:
9672 27/9/46.
69672 30/9/50.

CONDEMNED: 5/10/59.
Cut up at Stratford.

2633

Gorton.

To traffic 5/11/27.

REPAIRS:
Str. 26/10—18/12/29.**G.**
Str. 25/1—24/2/32.**G.**
Str. 4—5/8/32.**N/C.**
*Special fitting of tanks for
Lauritzen F.W. treatment*
Str. 2/3—19/4/34.**G.**
Str. 22/4—26/5/36.**G.**
Condensing gear removed.
Str. 10/6—2/7/38.**G.**
Str. 9/4—17/5/40.**G.**
Str. 1—13/6/41.**L.**
Str. 4/10—18/11/42.**G.**
Str. 22/4—31/5/45.**G.**
Str. 8/10—5/12/47.**G.**
Str. 1/1—4/2/50.**G.**
Altered to N7/3.
Str. 3/11—4/12/52.**G.**
Str. 3/10—15/11/55.**G.**
Str. 19—26/6/57.**N/C.**
Str. 30/12/57—16/1/58.**C/L.**
Str. 20—30/6/58.**C/L.**
Str. 29/9—31/10/58.**G.**
Str. 29/6—20/8/60.**C/L.**

BOILERS:
2046.
2112 24/2/32.
2090 19/4/34.
2026 26/5/36.
2090 2/7/38.
2032 17/5/40.
2033 18/11/42.
2019 31/5/45.
2038 5/12/47.
1931 4/2/50.
29053 4/12/52.
29080 15/11/55.
29120 31/10/58.

SHEDS:
Gorton.
Hatfield 8/12/27.
Stratford 21/1/29.
Colchester 15/3/53.
Parkeston 1/11/59.
Stratford 24/1/60.

RENUMBERED:
9673 30/11/46.
69673 4/2/50.

CONDEMNED: 10/9/61.
Cut up at Stratford.

2634

Gorton.

To traffic 14/11/27.

REPAIRS:
Str. 11/1—1/3/30.**G.**
Str. 19/3—29/4/32.**G.**
Str. 24/7—11/9/34.**G.**
Str. 15/6—13/7/36.**G.**
Condensing gear removed.
Str. 15/6—13/7/38.**G.**
Str. 27/6—13/8/40.**G.**
Str. 30/3—8/4/41.**L.**
Str. 17/1—18/3/43.**G.**
Str. 6/4—5/5/45.**G.**
Str. 16/11—18/12/47.**G.**
Str. 2/1—3/2/51.**G.**
Altered to N7/3.
Str. 13/11—19/12/53.**G.**
Str. 25/2—5/4/57.**G.**
Str. 27/11—17/12/58.**C/L.**
Str. 7—21/10/59.**C/L.**
Str. 30/12/59—5/2/60.**N/C.**
Str. 15/8—13/10/60.**C/L.**

BOILERS:
2047.
2053 29/4/32.
2054 11/9/34.
2028 13/7/36.
2112 13/7/38.
2090 13/8/40.

Black livery with red lining continued until November 1941 when war conditions caused cessation of lining. In 1927 the twenty built by Beardmore in Glasgow were sent south with their number at the rear on the bunker in Scottish Area style.

From June 1942 until into 1946, only NE instead of LNER was put on. Unlike the other works, Stratford continued to use $7\frac{1}{2}$in. size letters.

Other workshops began to restore LNER from early January 1946 but No.460, ex-Stratford on 2nd February 1946, still had only NE.

In the 1946 renumbering the hitherto random numbers on N7 Class were concentrated into 9600 to 9733. Because sheds made some of the changes, there were variations. No.2659 became 9699 on Monday 2nd September 1946 at Stratford and shows the care taken by someone from the works paint shop. Note the use of only 9in. high shaded transfers.

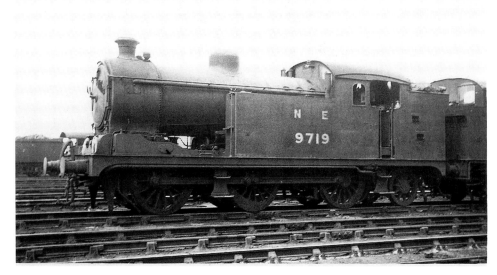

No.2617 changed to 9719 on Sunday 10th November 1946, also at Stratford shed, probably by shed staff as shown by the less meticulous spacing of the 9in. figures.

2634 cont./
  2020 18/3/43.
  2105 5/5/45.
  2006 18/12/47.
  29112 3/2/51.
  29130 *(new)* 19/12/53.
  29132 5/4/57.

SHEDS:
Gorton.
Hatfield 28/1/28.
Stratford 22/1/29.
Lincoln 15/6/49.
Boston 23/4/50.
Stratford 14/5/50.

RENUMBERED:
  9674 26/9/46.
  69674 3/2/51.

CONDEMNED: 12/6/61.
Cut up at Stratford.

_____

2635

Gorton.

To traffic 25/11/27.

REPAIRS:
Str. 21/3—16/5/30.**G.**
Str. 1/7—18/8/32.**G.**
Str. 28/10—18/11/32.**L.**
Str. 15/11/34—17/1/35.**L.**
Str. 7/3—20/4/37.**G.**
Condensing gear removed.
Str. 25/4—3/6/39.**G.**
Str. 6/4—20/5/41.**G.**
Str. 21/11/43—29/1/44.**G.**
Str. 30/8—29/9/46.**G.**
Altered to N7/3.
Str. 29/1—8/5/47.**L.**
Str. 10/6—30/7/49.**G.**
Str. 17/11—24/12/52.**G.**
Str. 18/5—10/6/55.**C/L.**
Str. 24/4—2/6/56.**G.**
Str. 5/8—17/9/59.**G.**
Str. 24—30/9/59.**N/C.**
Str. 13—14/10/59.**N/C.**

BOILERS:
  2048.
  2039 18/8/32.
  2044 17/1/35.
  2092 20/4/37.
  2017 3/6/39.
   989 20/5/41.
  2037 29/1/44.
  1980 29/9/46.
  1975 30/7/49.
  29049 24/12/52.
  29106 2/6/56.
  29007 17/9/59.

SHEDS:
Gorton.
Hatfield 11/1/28.
Stratford 23/1/29.
Lincoln 8/9/49.
Stratford 23/4/50.
Parkeston 28/10/56.
Stratford 24/1/60.

RENUMBERED:
  9675 30/11/46.
  69675 30/7/49.

CONDEMNED: 26/6/61.
Cut up at Stratford.

_____

2636

Gorton.

To traffic 10/12/27.

REPAIRS:
Str. 18/12/29—22/2/30.**G.**
Str. 9/1—12/3/32.**G.**
Str. 16/5—28/6/34.**G.**
Str. 7/9—7/10/36.**G.**
Condensing gear removed.
Str. 22/6—22/7/38.**G.**
Str. 23/8—16/9/38.**L.**
Str. 13/8—30/10/40.**G.**
Str. 23/12/42—6/2/43.**G.**
Str. 7/3—29/4/44.**G.**
Str. 14/7—1/9/46.**G.**
Altered to N7/3.
Str. 1/9—8/10/49.**G.**
Str. 9/5—26/6/52.**G.**
Str. 20/9—1/10/54.**C/L.**
Str. 6/12/55—28/1/56.**G.**
Str. 8—14/2/56.**N/C.**
Str. 27/8—13/9/57.**C/L.**

BOILERS:
  2049.
  2008 12/3/32.
   980 28/6/34.
  2050 7/10/36.
  2029 22/7/38.
  2104 30/10/40.
  2113 29/4/44.
  2076 1/9/46.
  1940 8/10/49.
  29070 26/6/52.
  29012 28/1/56.

SHEDS:
Gorton.
Hatfield 11/1/28.
Stratford 25/1/29.
Colchester 19/4/47.
Stratford 7/6/47.

RENUMBERED:
  9676 30/8/46.

69676 8/10/49.

CONDEMNED: 16/2/59.
Cut up at Stratford.

_____

2637

Gorton.

To traffic 21/12/27.

REPAIRS:
Str. 17/5—22/7/30.**G.**
Str. 18/7—13/9/32.**G.**
Str. 6/11—31/12/34.**G.**
Str. 10/1—19/2/37.**G.**
Condensing gear removed.
Str. 11/12/38—19/1/39.**G.**
Str. 3/11—1/12/39.**L.**
Str. 9/1—7/2/40.**G.**
Str. 30/5—12/7/41.**G.**
Str. 24/3—4/5/44.**G.**
Str. 29/8—14/11/46.**G.**
Altered to N7/3.
Str. 31/5—2/7/49.**G.**
Str. 20/1—24/2/50.**C/L.**
Str. 14/12/50—6/1/51.**C/L.**
Str. 1/8—13/9/52.**G.**
Str. 18/10—26/11/55.**G.**
Str. 18—26/6/57.**C/L.**
Str. 24/3—9/5/58.**C/L.**
Str. 18/9—24/10/58.**G.**
Str. 25/2—20/3/59.**C/L.**
Str. 11/4—20/5/60.**C/L.**

BOILERS:
  2050.
  2043 13/9/32.
  2007 31/12/34.
  2115 19/2/37.
  2028 19/1/39.
  2041 12/7/41.
  2050 4/5/44.
  1913 14/11/46.
  1956 2/7/49.
  1956 reno.29016 6/1/51.
  29077 13/9/52.
  29121 26/11/55.
  29005 24/10/58.

SHEDS:
Gorton.
Hatfield 29/2/28.
Stratford 19/4/29.
Parkeston 4/12/49.
Stratford 27/7/52.

RENUMBERED:
  9677 9/11/46.
  69677 2/7/49.

CONDEMNED: 24/11/60.
Cut up at Stratford.

_____

2638

Gorton.

To traffic 7/1/28.

REPAIRS:
Str. 25/1—15/3/30.**G.**
Str. 9/7—24/8/32.**G.**
Str. 4/9—26/10/34.**G.**
Str. 24/10—20/11/36.**G.**
Condensing gear removed.
Str. 11/12/38—13/1/39.**G.**
Str. 23/2—4/4/41.**G.**
Str. 6/11—18/12/43.**G.**
Altered to N7/3.
Str. 5—26/2/46.**G.**
Str. 7/11—11/12/48.**G.**
Str. 7/12/50—27/1/51.**G.**
Str. 22/12/53—23/1/54.**G.**
Str. 11—25/8/54.**C/L.**
Str. 22/11—16/12/55.**C/L.**
Str. 30/5—28/7/56.**G.**
Str. 29/7—5/9/59.**G.**

BOILERS:
  2051.
  2005 24/8/32.
  2041 26/10/34.
  2006 20/11/36.
  2091 13/1/39.
  2118 4/4/41.
  2074 18/12/43.
  1970 26/2/46.
  1945 11/12/48.
  29111 27/1/51.
  29004 23/1/54.
  29105 28/7/56.
  29067 5/9/59.

SHEDS:
Gorton.
Hatfield 28/1/28.
Stratford 18/4/29.
Colchester 8/7/51.
Stratford 23/9/51.
Colchester 11/11/51.
Hatfield 14/9/52.
Stratford 21/8/60.

RENUMBERED:
  9678 28/9/46.
  69678 4/12/48.

CONDEMNED: 10/9/61.
Cut up at Stratford.

_____

2639

Gorton.

To traffic 24/1/28.

No.7995 did not become 9617 until Friday 3rd January 1947 also at Stratford shed. The 12in. high painted and unshaded figures bear evidence of application by someone from the paint shop.

No.2650 had LNER restored ex-works from general repair on 20th June 1946. It was changed to 9690 on Sunday 27th October 1946 at Hatfield shed in 12in. unshaded figures by a local painter.

No.2609 became 9711 from 6th September 1946 but LNER was only restored when ex-works on 14th April 1947 and for its number Stratford was able to find 12in. shaded transfers.

2639 cont./

REPAIRS:
Str. 31/5—15/8/30.**G.**
Str. 12/9—7/10/32.**G.**
Str. 8/8—10/10/34.**G.**
Str. 22/9—16/10/36.**G.**
Condensing gear removed.
Str. 28/11—15/12/37.**H.**
Str. 20—28/12/37.**L.**
Str. 9/10—11/11/38.**G.**
Str. 29/3—20/4/40.**G.**
Str. 9/12/40—22/1/41.**G.**
Str. 11/10—7/12/42.**L/I.**
Str. 30/11/43—14/1/44.**G.**
Altered to N7/3.
Str. 2/1—1/2/46.**G.**
Str. 9—20/12/47.**L.**
Str. 15/8—28/9/48.**G.**
Tablet Exch. App. fitted.
Str. 21/1—17/2/51.**G.**
Str. 17—31/7/52.**C/L.**
Str. 7/2—12/3/54.**G.**
Str. 31/3—10/5/57.**G.**
Westinghouse brake removed.
Steam brake fitted.
Push-pull gear fitted.

BOILERS:
 2052.
 2050 7/10/32.
 2025 10/10/34.
 982 16/10/36.
 989 15/12/37.
 980 11/11/38.
 2114 20/4/40.
 2074 14/1/44.
 2082 1/2/46.
 1982 28/9/48.
 29021 17/2/51.
 29111 12/3/54.
 29019 10/5/57.

SHEDS:
Gorton.
Hatfield 29/2/28.
Stratford 17/4/29.
Ipswich 10/10/48.
Melton Constable 8/12/48.
Norwich 10/9/50.
Lowestoft 8/7/56.
Yarmouth 19/5/57.
Stratford 6/10/57.
Tilbury 3/11/57.
Yarmouth 8/3/58.
Stratford 1/2/59.
Parkeston 20/11/60.
Stratford 1/1/61.

RENUMBERED:
 9679 30/11/46.
69679 25/9/48.

CONDEMNED: 17/1/61.
Cut up at Stratford.

2640

Gorton.

To traffic 6/2/28.

REPAIRS:
Don. 9/11/29—9/1/30.**G.**
Don. 20/2—12/4/32.**G.**
Str. 5/6—6/7/34.**G.**
Str. 19/4—18/5/36.**G.**
Str. 9/9—6/10/37.**G.**
Condensing gear removed.
Str. 3—12/5/38.**L.**
Str. 25/4—4/5/39.**L.**
Str. 21/6—4/8/39.**G.**
Str. 20/10/40—3/1/41.**G.**
Str. 14/3—3/4/41.**L.**
Str. 11/4—16/5/42.**G.**
Str. 8/8—16/9/44.**L.**
Str. 25/2—26/3/45.**G.**
Str. 5/1—28/2/47.**G.**
Str. 18/8—22/9/49.**G.**
Altered to N7/3.
Str. 29/9—3/10/49.**N/C.**
Str. 11/2—29/3/52.**G.**
Str. 26/7—28/8/54.**G.**
Str. 11—20/10/56.**N/C.**
Str. 28/1—2/3/57.**G.**
Str. 27/5—27/6/59.**G.**

BOILERS:
 2053.
 2025 12/4/32.
 2049 6/7/34.
 2114 18/5/36.
 2030 6/10/37.
 2098 4/8/39.
 2035 3/1/41.
 2116 16/5/42.
 2088 26/3/45.
 2017 28/2/47.
 1964 22/9/49.
 29059 29/3/52.
 29132 *(new)* 28/8/54.
 29145 2/3/57.
 29134 27/6/59.

SHEDS:
Gorton.
Hatfield 8/5/28.
Stratford 9/1/30.

RENUMBERED:
 9680 28/9/46.
69680 22/9/49.

CONDEMNED: 4/12/60.
Cut up at Stratford.

2641

Gorton.

To traffic 28/2/28.

REPAIRS:
Don. 7/12/29—27/1/30.**G.**
Str. 11/6—9/8/32.**G.**
Str. 6/9—18/10/34.**G.**
Str. 30/4—5/6/36.**G.**
Condensing gear removed.
Str. 28/11—30/12/37.**G.**
Str. 13/8—29/9/39.**G.**
Str. 20/4—9/5/41.**L.**
Str. 6/7—16/8/41.**G.**
Str. 3—18/2/42.**L.**
Str. 10—29/6/42.**L.**
Str. 7/5—16/7/43.**G.**
Str. 23/1—6/3/45.**G.**
Str. 2/6—2/8/47.**G.**
Str. 4/8—24/9/49.**G.**
Str. 13/3—26/4/52.**G.**
Altered to N7/3.
Str. 18/10—20/11/54.**G.**
Str. 27/9—12/10/56.**C/L.**
Str. 15/2—16/3/57.**G.**
Str. 14/3—21/4/60.**C/L.**
Str. 31/5—10/6/60.**C/L.**

BOILERS:
 2054.
 2006 9/8/32.
 987 18/10/34.
 2021 5/6/36.
 2095 31/12/37.
 2053 29/9/39.
 2010 16/8/41.
 2088 2/8/47.
 2114 24/9/49.
 29063 26/4/52.
 29042 20/11/54.
 29107 16/3/57.

SHEDS:
Gorton.
Hatfield 8/5/28.
Stratford 25/1/30.

RENUMBERED:
 9681 15/12/46.
69681 24/9/49.

CONDEMNED: 4/12/60.
Cut up at Stratford.

2642

W. Beardmore 305.

To traffic 29/6/27.

REPAIRS:
Str. ?/?—25/5/29.**G.**
Additional handrail to Drawing
26568E fitted 29/8/29.
Str. 22/11/30—9/1/31.**G.**
Str. 17/12/32—19/1/33.**G.**
Str. 18—20/6/34.**L.**
Str. 3/11/34—5/1/35.**G.**
Condensing gear removed.
Str. 25/9—22/10/36.**G.**
Str. 3/11—14/12/38.**G.**
Steam brake removed.
Westinghouse brake fitted.
Str. 12/1—6/3/41.**G.**
Str. 14/10—16/11/42.**L.**
Str. 19/12/43—5/2/44.**G.**
Str. 27/2—22/3/46.**G.**
Altered to N7/3.
Str. 5/12/47—8/1/48.**H.**
Str. 26/9—10/11/48.**G.**
Str. 4—31/3/51.**G.**
Str. 24/10—11/11/52.**C/L.**
Str. 24/6—6/8/53.**G.**
Str. 7/11—17/12/55.**G.**
Str. 29/7—9/8/57.**C/L.**
Str. 3/6—25/7/58.**G.**
Str. 23/5—1/7/60.**C/L.**

BOILERS:
 2087.
 2117 9/1/31.
 2017 19/1/33.
 2115 5/1/35.
 2091 22/10/36.
 2041 14/12/38.
 2113 6/3/41.
 989 5/2/44.
 1986 22/3/46.
 1947 10/11/48.
 29114 *(new)* 31/3/51.
 29044 6/8/53.
 29120 17/12/55.
 29138 25/7/58.

SHEDS:
King's Cross.
Hatfield 27/11/28.
Stratford 14/12/38.

RENUMBERED:
 9682 20/10/46.
69682 6/11/48.

CONDEMNED: 4/12/60.
Cut up at Stratford.

LNER was restored to No.2642 ex-works 22nd March 1946 and when changed to 9682 on Sunday 20th October 1946 in 9in. shaded transfers, skilled attention is clear, especially from care taken on the front buffer beam.

By 14th July 1947, when No.9720 was ex-works, shaded transfers had to give way to yellow painted and unshaded characters. These were nominally in Gill sans but the 9 was the modified LNER version.

Stratford economised on painting to the greatest possible degree. Although ex-works 10th January 1948, No.9639 still carried LNER and in shaded transfers. Out from a light repair on 13th April 1948 it had been given its BR number and in the shaded transfers on tank sides. For the five-figure number on the front buffer beam there was insufficient space for the corresponding $4^{1}/_{2}$in. shaded transfers so the number was unshaded there.

9703 had LNER again ex-works 27th May 1947 and in shaded transfers. From a light repair on 5th April 1948 it had acquired its BR number and still in 12in. shaded transfers.

2643

W. Beardmore 306.

To traffic 2/7/27.

REPAIRS:
Str. 11/3—7/6/29.**G.**
Str. 24/4—19/6/31.**G.**
Str. 4/5—8/6/33.**G.**
Str. 21/2—10/4/35.**G.**
Str. 28/3—11/5/37.**G.**
Str. 3/2—4/3/39.**H.**
Str. 24/8—15/9/39.**G.**
Str. 12/3—27/4/40.**L.**
Steam brake removed.
Westinghouse brake fitted.
Str. 20/2—17/4/42.**G.**
Additional washout plugs fitted.
Str. 26/10—10/12/43.**G.**
Str. 22/5—26/6/45.**G.**
Str. 16/10—6/12/47.**G.**
Str. 9/4—20/5/50.**G.**
Str. 20/10—28/11/52.**G.**
Str. 24/3—5/4/54.**C/L.**
Str. 16/11—24/12/54.**G.**
Altered to N7/3.
Str. 19/7—24/8/55.**C/L.**
Str. 18/3—2/5/57.**G.**
Str. 26/8—5/9/58.**C/L.**
Str. 19—20/1/60. *Not repaired.*
Str. 9/2/60. *Not repaired.*

BOILERS:
2088.
2027 19/6/31.
2032 8/6/33.
2024 10/4/35.
2043 11/5/37.
2038 4/3/39.
2044 17/4/42.
2048 26/6/45.
2120 6/12/47.
27862 28/11/52.
29115 24/12/54.
29031 2/5/57.

SHEDS:
King's Cross.
Hatfield 28/11/28.
King's Cross 7/7/29.
Hatfield 9/1/30.
Stratford 27/4/40.

RENUMBERED:
9683 6/10/46.
69683 20/5/50.

CONDEMNED: 15/2/60.
Cut up at Stratford.

2644

W. Beardmore 307.

To traffic 6/7/27.

REPAIRS:
Str. ?/?—11/5/29.**G.**
Str. 8/12/30—12/2/31.**G.**
Str. 12/11—31/12/32.**G.**
Str. 24—26/9/34.**L.**
Str. 9/11/34—9/1/35.**G.**
Condensing gear removed.
Str. 7/10—11/11/36.**G.**
Str. 15/12/38—1/2/39.**G.**
Steam brake removed.
Westinghouse brake fitted.
Str. 31/1—14/3/41.**G.**
Str. 21/4—1/5/42.**L.**
Str. 28—30/5/42.**L.**
Str. 12/9—23/10/43.**G.**
Str. 2—22/9/45.**G.**
Str. 28/12/47—23/2/48.**G.**
Str. 23/3—20/5/50.**G.**
Altered to N7/3.
Str. 17/7—3/8/51.**C/L.**
Str. 12—18/6/52.**C/L.**
Str. 2/10—8/11/52.**G.**
Str. 28/2—2/4/55.**G.**
Str. 4—13/12/56.**C/L.**
Str. 12/6—9/8/57.**G.**
Str. 19/7/60. *Not repaired.*

BOILERS:
2089.
984 12/2/31.
2024 31/12/32.
2103 9/1/35.
2010 11/11/36.
2012 1/2/39.
2018 14/3/41.
2106 23/10/43.
2096 22/9/45.
2020 23/2/48.
1987 20/5/50.
1987 reno.29038 3/8/51.
29097 *(new)* 2/4/55.
29042 9/8/57.

SHEDS:
King's Cross.
Hatfield 29/11/28.
Stratford 3/6/38.
Hatfield 3/11/38.
Stratford 1/2/39.

RENUMBERED:
9684 15/12/46.
ᴇ**9684** 23/2/48.
69684 20/5/50.

CONDEMNED: 29/8/60.
Cut up at Stratford.

2645

W. Beardmore 308.

To traffic 13/7/27.

REPAIRS:
Str. ?/?—10/7/29.**G.**
Str. 4/7—5/9/31.**G.**
Str. 4/9—13/10/33.**G.**
Str. 1/11—4/12/35.**G.**
Str. 26/11/37—3/1/38.**G.**
Steam brake removed.
Westinghouse brake fitted.
Str. 4/11—13/12/39.**G.**
Str. 10/2—3/4/42.**G.**
Additional washout plugs fitted.
Str. 12/11—21/12/44.**G.**
Str. 20/8—10/10/47.**G.**
Altered to N7/3.
Str. 2—31/8/49.**C/L.**
Str. 20/11—23/12/49.**G.**
Str. 10/3—6/5/52.**G.**
Str. 11/3—15/4/54.**G.**
Str. 26/6—15/8/56.**C/L.**
Str. 13/1—16/2/57.**G.**
Str. 3/3—8/4/60.**C/L.**

BOILERS:
2090.
2105 13/10/33.
2113 4/12/35.
2019 3/1/38.
2022 13/12/39.
2006 3/4/42.
2099 21/12/44.
1962 10/10/47.
1935 23/12/49.
29064 6/5/52.
29033 15/4/54.
29146 16/2/57.

SHEDS:
King's Cross.
Hatfield 10/12/28.
Stratford 3/1/38.

RENUMBERED:
9685 18/10/46.
69685 23/12/49.

CONDEMNED: 4/12/60.
Cut up at Stratford.

2646

W. Beardmore 309.

To traffic 23/727.

REPAIRS:
Str. 26/3—19/6/29.**G.**
Str. 18/2—9/5/31.**G.**
Str. 12/11/32—6/1/33.**G.**

Str. 2—5/6/34.**L.**
Str. 1/1—11/2/35.**G.**
Str. 2/3—21/4/37.**G.**
Condensing gear removed.
Str. 3/2—18/3/39.**G.**
Steam brake removed.
Westinghouse brake fitted.
Str. 12/3—19/4/41.**G.**
Str. 27—28/5/42.**L.**
Str. 17/10—18/12/43.**G.**
Altered to N7/3.
Str. 15/10—10/11/45.**G.**
Str. 2/5—9/6/47.**L.**
Str. 16/5—24/6/48.**G.**
Str. 7/9—20/10/50.**G.**
Str. 2/2—7/3/53.**G.**
Str. 14/1—5/2/55.**C/L.**
Str. 21/2—29/3/56.**G.**
Str. 30/7—16/8/57.**C/L.**
Str. 21/11—24/12/57.**C/L.**
Str. 26/8—26/9/58.**G.**
Str. 3—18/3/60.**N/C.**

BOILERS:
2091.
2094 6/1/33.
2043 11/2/35.
2093 21/4/37.
2013 18/3/39.
2016 19/4/41.
2082 18/12/43.
1966 10/11/45.
1926 24/6/48.
29008 20/10/50.
29123 *(new)* 7/3/53.
29108 29/3/56.
29143 26/9/58.

SHEDS:
King's Cross.
Hatfield 24/1/29.
Stratford 18/3/39.
Colchester 25/1/59.
Stratford 3/5/59.
Parkeston 24/7/60.
Stratford 16/10/60.

RENUMBERED:
9686 14/12/46.
69686 19/6/48.

CONDEMNED: 10/9/61.
Cut up at Stratford.

2647

W. Beardmore 310.

To traffic 22/7/27.

REPAIRS:
Str. ?/?—?/7/29.**G.**
Str. ?/?—?/12/32.**G.**
Str. ?/?—?/1/35.**G.**

2647 cont./
Str. ?/?—18/12/36.**G.**
Str. ?/?—24/11/38.**G.**
Steam brake removed.
Westinghouse brake fitted.
Str. ?/?—17/12/40.**G.**
Str. ?/?—13/11/42.**G.**
Str. ?/?—?/12/44.**G.**
Altered to N7/3.
Str. 29/3—10/5/47.**G.**
Str. 18/8—10/9/49.**G.**
Str. 3/12/51—16/1/52.**G.**
Str. 19/3—10/4/53.**C/L.**
Str. 26/5—26/6/54.**G.**
Str. 5—26/7/56.**C/L.**
Str. 21/1—23/2/57.**G.**
Str. 23/6—15/8/59.**G.**

BOILERS:
  2092.
  2052 ?/12/32.
  2013 ?/1/35.
  2118 18/12/36.
  2025 24/11/38.
  2036 17/12/40.
  2078 ?/12/44.
  2060 10/5/47.
  1957 10/9/49.
29054 16/1/52.
29064 26/6/54.
29142 23/2/57.
29032 15/8/59.

SHEDS:
King's Cross.
Hatfield 22/9/29.
Stratford 25/11/38.

RENUMBERED:
  9687 3/10/46.
69687 10/9/49.

CONDEMNED: 4/12/60.
Cut up at Stratford.

From a general repair on 9th September 1947, No.9625 had Gill sans characters, so when ex-works 23rd December 1948 from light repair, it got BR number 69625 also in unshaded Gill sans and with correct 6 and 9. The figures were 10in. tall, which by then, had become the standard height.

Between 17th January and 24th March 1948, eleven N7 had the regional prefix E added to their number. These were E9600 (4th March), E9610 (28th February), E9640 (4th March), E9652 (21st February), E9654 (21st February), E9657 (19th March), E9658 (24th January), E9668 (18th February), E9684 (23rd February), E9697 (24th March), and E9717 (17th January).

This first essay to show the new ownership kept 7$\frac{1}{2}$in. letters and 12in. figures in the same positions as the LNER had used. Both were in painted, unshaded Gill sans but with the LNER modification to 6 and 9.

2648

W. Beardmore 311.

To traffic 22/7/27.

REPAIRS:
Str. ?/?—25/5/29.**G.**
Str. 6/2—13/5/31.**G.**
Str. 12/11—23/12/32.**G.**
Str. 7/10—24/11/33.**G.**
Str. 29/6—21/8/35.**G.**
Str. 3/8—4/9/37.**G.**
Str. 29/9—9/11/39.**G.**
Steam brake removed.
Westinghouse brake fitted.
Str. 7/2—18/3/42.**G.**
Str. 17/3—29/4/44.**G.**
Str. 21/2—22/3/46.**G.**
Str. 29/8—12/10/48.**G.**
Str. 26/4—5/5/49.**C/L.**
Str. 24/3—3/5/50.**C/L.**
Str. 18/3—26/4/51.**G.**
Altered to N7/3.
Str. 23/7—5/9/53.**G.**
Str. 21—28/10/53.**N/C.**
Str. 3/4—12/5/56.**G.**
Str. 1/7—8/8/57.**C/L.**
Str. 3—12/2/58.**C/L.**
Str. 1/10—7/11/58.**G.**

BOILERS:
 2093.
 2021 23/12/32.
 2019 24/11/33.
  984 21/8/35.
 2033 4/9/37.
 2039 9/11/39.
 2017 18/3/42.
 2087 29/4/44.
 2012 22/3/46.
 2032 12/10/48.
29027 26/4/51.
29083 5/9/53.
29053 12/5/56.
29098 7/11/58.

SHEDS:
King's Cross.
Hatfield 26/1/29.
Stratford 12/11/39.

RENUMBERED:
 9688 6/10/46.
69688 9/10/48.

CONDEMNED: 24/11/60.
Cut up at Stratford.

2649

W. Beardmore 312.

To traffic 3/8/27.

REPAIRS:
Str. 17/3—15/6/29.**G.**
Str. 8/6—12/8/31.**G.**
Str. 25/1—11/3/33.**G.**
Str. 11—17/7/34.**L.**
Str. 29/1—8/3/35.**G.**
Str. 5/2—12/3/37.**G.**
Str. 9—27/7/37.**L.**
Str. 25/7—16/9/39.**G.**
Str. 25/4—14/6/42.**G.**
Str. 9/11—18/12/43.**L.**
Str. 7/11—1/12/45.**G.**
Str. 10/2—28/6/47.**G.**
Str. 4/1—24/2/49.**G.**
Push-pull gear fitted.
Str. 10—30/6/49.**C/L.**
Str. 29/10—1/12/51.**G.**
Str. 8—21/6/52.**N/C.**
Str. 21/4—4/6/55.**C/L.**
Str. 26/2—29/3/56.**C/L.**
Str. 6/7—3/8/56.**C/L.**
Str. 1/3/57. *Not repaired.*

BOILERS:
 2094.
 2099 12/8/31.
 2117 11/3/33.
 2017 8/3/35.
 2014 12/3/37.
 2120 16/9/39.
 2121 14/6/42.
 2090 1/12/45.
 2011 24/2/49.
27857 1/12/51.

SHEDS:
King's Cross.
Hatfield 22/1/29.
King's Cross 7/7/29.
Hatfield 9/1/30.
Bradford 21/6/42.
Hatfield 9/10/43.
Neasden 3/7/49.
King's Cross 1/7/51.
Annesley 30/5/54.
Yarmouth 27/2/55.

RENUMBERED:
 9689 16/12/46.
69689 24/2/49.

CONDEMNED: 25/3/57.
Cut up at Stratford.

2650

W Beardmore 313.

To traffic 6/8/27.

REPAIRS:
Str. 13/5—24/8/29.**G.**
Str. 25/4—3/7/31.**G.**
Str. 14/11—5/12/32.**L.**
Str. 8/7—18/8/33.**G.**
Str. 3—10/5/34.**L.**
Str. 8/6—24/7/35.**G.**
Condensing gear removed.
Str. 4/8—7/9/37.**G.**
Str. 14/8—2/10/39.**G.**
Str. 31/1—12/4/43.**G.**
Str. 25/4—1/5/43.**N/C.**
Str. 2—9/5/43.**N/C.**
Str. 6/5—20/6/46.**G.**
Str. 28/4—28/5/49.**G.**
Str. 30/5—1/6/49.**N/C.**
Push-pull gear fitted.
Str. 11—28/6/49.**C/L.**
Str. 20/6—1/9/51.**G.**
Str. 27/4—15/5/53.**N/C.**
Str. 27/11/54—8/1/55.**G.**
Altered to N7/3.
Str. 15—24/1/57.**N/C.**
Str. 5/12/57—16/1/58.**G.**
Str. 23/9—2/10/58.**C/L.**
Str. 31/5—3/8/60.**C/L.**

BOILERS:
 2095.
 2088 18/8/33.
 2030 24/7/35.
 2009 7/9/37.
 2011 2/10/39.
 2034 12/4/43.
 2119 20/6/46.
 2090 28/5/49.
27855 1/9/51.
29119 8/1/55.
29051 16/1/58.

SHEDS:
King's Cross.
Hatfield 25/2/29.
Bradford 16/1/42.
Hatfield 5/1/44.
Neasden 3/7/49.
King's Cross 9/9/51.
Norwich 15/3/53.
Lowestoft 10/6/56.
Cambridge 30/9/56.
Lowestoft 20/7/58.
Stratford 12/4/59.
Parkeston 24/1/60.
Stratford 1/1/61.

RENUMBERED:
 9690 27/10/46.
69690 28/5/49.

CONDEMNED: 13/1/61.

2651

W Beardmore 314.

To traffic 10/8/27.

REPAIRS:
Str. 4/7—13/9/29.**G.**
Str. 25/7—19/9/31.**G.**
Str. 24/10—17/11/33.**G.**
Str. 4—6/7/34.**L.**
Str. 10/5—21/6/35.**G.**
Str. 8/5—11/6/37.**G.**
Condensing gear removed.
Str. 9/7—24/8/39.**G.**
Str. 15/2—11/3/42.**G.**
Str. 25/2—25/4/45.**G.**
Altered to N7/3.
Str. 12/10—26/11/47.**G.**
Str. 10/9—13/10/50.**G.**
Str. 9—29/9/51.**N/C.**
Push-pull gear fitted.
Str. 3—29/8/53.**G.**
Str. 5/3—27/5/54.**C/L.**
Str. 17/8—28/9/56.**G.**
Str. 12/8—30/9/60.**C/L.**

BOILERS:
 2096.
 2022 19/9/31.
 2023 17/11/33.
 2117 21/6/35.
 2102 11/6/37.
 2094 24/8/39.
 2040 11/3/42.
 1930 25/4/45.
 1916 26/11/47.
29009 13/10/50.
29019 29/8/53.
29094 28/9/56.

SHEDS:
King's Cross.
Stratford 16/8/27.
King's Cross 24/8/27.
Hatfield 27/1/30.
Bradford 6/1/42.
Hatfield 19/1/44.
Annesley 4/11/51.
Ardsley 30/5/54.
Copley Hill 3/10/54.
Plaistow 18/12/55.
Tilbury 17/9/56.
Stratford 3/11/57.

WORKS CODES:- Cw - Cowlairs. Dar- Darlington. Doncaster. Ghd - Gateshead. Gor - Gorton. Inv - Inverurie. Str- Stratford.
REPAIR CODES:- **C/H** - Casual Heavy. **C/L** - Casual Light. **G** - General. **H**- Heavy. **H/I** - Heavy Intermediate. **L** - Light. **L/I** - Light Intermediate. **N/C** - Non-Classified.

71

There was a small change on the last two to get the E prefix, both in March 1948, the numerals on E9657 (19th) and E9697 (24th), being only 10in. tall.

The same positions and sizes were continued for the full BR number which superseded the E prefix, at least to 2nd July 1948, when 69647 was ex-works.

By the time 69664 was ex-works 13th August 1948, the number had been moved to the bunker. BRITISH RAILWAYS had been centred on the tank with both in matching 10in. on the same level and with correct Gill sans 6 and 9. Note, the offset number caused by the single sunken footstep.

2651 cont./
Parkeston 24/1/60.
Stratford 24/7/60.

RENUMBERED:
 9691 11/8/46.
69691 13/10/50.

CONDEMNED: 4/12/60.
Cut up at Stratford.

_____

2652

W Beardmore 315.

To traffic 16/8/27.

REPAIRS:
Str. 1/3—1/6/29.**G.**
Str. 8/1—19/2/31.**G.**
Str. 12/11/32—9/1/33.**G.**
Str. 18/12/34—4/2/35.**G.**
Str. 21/2—24/3/37.**G.**
Str. 4/4—1/6/39.**G.**
Str. 10/4—15/5/41.**G.**
Str. 24/6—12/8/44.**G.**
Altered to N7/3.
Str. 7/3—13/4/46.**G.**
Str. 5—23/10/46.**L.**
Str. 7/8—29/9/48.**G.**
Str. 17/6—1/7/49.**C/L.**
Push-pull gear fitted.
Str. 5/3—7/4/51.**G.**
Str. 10/9—4/10/52.**C/L.**
Str. 18/6—20/8/55.**G.**
Str. 30/12/56—9/1/57.**N/C.**
Str. 10/3—18/4/58.**G.**
Str. 25/2—20/3/59.**C/L.**

BOILERS:
 2097.
 2092 9/1/33.
 2093 4/2/35.
 2098 24/3/37.
 2103 1/6/39.
 2098 15/5/41.
 1955 12/8/44.
 1975 13/4/46.
 1938 29/9/48.
29025 7/4/51.
29065 20/8/55.
29024 18/4/58.

SHEDS:
King's Cross.
Hatfield 18/1/29.
Bradford 8/1/42.
Hatfield 2/11/43.
Neasden 3/7/49.
King's Cross 13/7/51.
Annesley 16/5/54.
Stratford 17/10/54.
Annesley 14/11/54.
Copley Hill 6/2/55.

Annesley 13/2/55.
Cambridge 30/9/56.
Stratford 17/8/58.
Hatfield 29/3/59.
King's Cross 1/1/61.
Stratford 9/4/61.

RENUMBERED:
 9692 11/8/46.
69692 29/9/48.

CONDEMNED: 16/9/62.

_____

2653

W Beardmore 316.

To traffic 17/8/27.

REPAIRS:
Str. 10/5—24/8/29.**G.**
Str. 12/9—7/11/31.**G.**
Str. 7—31/7/33.**L.**
Steam brake removed.
Westinghouse brake fitted.
Str. 6/10—29/11/34.**G.**
Str. 11/12/36—21/1/37.**G.**
Condensing gear removed.
Str. 6/1—8/2/39.**G.**
Str. 1/12/40—4/1/41.**G.**
Str. 3—24/4/41.**L.**
Str. 13/9—29/10/43.**G.**
Str. 21/3—23/4/46.**G.**
Altered to N7/3.
Str. 12/12/48—20/1/49.**G.**
Str. 22—23/1/49.**N/C.**
Str. 7/12/50—20/1/51.**G.**
Str. 11—22/11/52.**C/L.**
Str. 31/3—9/5/53.**G.**
Str. 25/8—13/10/55.**G.**
Str. 13/10—28/12/56.**N/C.**
Str. 29/7—30/8/57.**C/L.**
Str. 6/8—11/9/58.**G.**
Str. 21/7—26/8/60.**C/L.**

BOILERS:
 2098.
 2103 7/11/31.
 2098 29/11/34.
 2047 21/1/37.
 989 8/2/39.
 2029 4/1/41.
 2045 29/10/43.
 1976 23/4/46.
 1986 20/1/49.
29110 20/1/51.
29001 9/5/53.
29092 13/10/55.
29037 11/9/58.

SHEDS:
King's Cross.
Cambridge 30/3/33.
King's Cross 29/5/33.

Stratford 10/6/33.

RENUMBERED:
 9693 17/4/46.
69693 15/1/49.

CONDEMNED: 10/9/61.

_____

2654

W Beardmore 317.

To traffic 18/8/27.

REPAIRS:
Str. 24/7—8/10/29.**G.**
Str. 30/5—10/7/31.**G.**
Str. 14/11—8/12/32.**L.**
Str. 12/5—23/6/33.**G.**
Str. 19—23/5/34.**L.**
Str. 6/7—30/8/35.**G.**
Str. 22/8—17/9/37.**G.**
Str. 6/11—16/12/39.**G.**
Str. 20/11—?/12/42.**G.**
Str. 10/10—17/11/45.**G.**
Str. 11/5—25/6/48.**G.**
Str. 8—19/8/49.**C/L.**
Push-pull gear fitted.
Str. 29/10—7/12/50.**G.**
Str. 5/10—6/11/54.**G.**
Altered to N7/3.
Str. 29/7—16/8/57.**C/L.**
Str. 21/3—27/5/60.**C/L.**

BOILERS:
 2099.
 2088 10/7/31.
 2034 23/6/33.
 2032 30/8/35.
 2015 17/9/37.
 2034 16/12/39.
 2023 ?/12/42.
 2106 17/11/45.
 2049 25/6/48.
27851 7/12/50.
29023 6/11/54.

SHEDS:
King's Cross.
Hatfield 25/1/29.
Bradford 21/1/42.
Hatfield 7/10/43.
Lincoln 15/10/48.
Boston 31/10/48.
Hatfield 12/12/48.
Neasden 21/8/49.
King's Cross 15/7/51.
Ardsley 6/6/54.
Copley Hill 3/10/54.
Tilbury 4/11/56.
King's Lynn 3/3/58.
Stratford 17/7/60.
Parkeston 16/10/60.

RENUMBERED:
 9694 11/8/48.
69694 25/6/48.

CONDEMNED: 24/11/60.
Cut up at Stratford.

_____

2655

W Beardmore 318.

To traffic 24/8/27.

REPAIRS:
Str. 9—30/11/28.**G.**
Str. 27/7—12/10/29.**G.**
Str. 27/6—27/8/31.**G.**
Str. 5/11—15/12/32.**G.**
Str. 23/9—22/11/34.**G.**
Str. 17/11/36—5/1/37.**G.**
Condensing gear removed.
Str. 4/3—13/4/39.**G.**
Str. 23/8—28/9/41.**G.**
Don. 3/9—14/10/44.**G.**
Str. 2/12/47—20/1/48.**G.**
Str. 25/5—19/6/48.**L.**
Derailed at St. Albans.
Str. 19/1—24/2/51.**G.**
Str. 7—24/10/51.**N/C.**
Push-pull gear fitted.
Str. 1/3—9/4/54.**C/L.**
Str. 13/12/54—22/1/55.**G.**
Str. 13—23/12/55.**C/L.**
Str. 11—18/4/57.**C/L.**
Str. 27/11/58. *Not repaired.*

BOILERS:
 2100.
 2094 27/8/31.
 2013 15/12/32.
 2033 22/11/34.
 2040 5/1/37.
 2006 13/4/39.
 2046 28/9/41.
 2019 20/1/48.
27853 24/2/51.
27855 22/1/55.

SHEDS:
King's Cross.
Hatfield 5/12/28.
King's Cross 20/2/35.
Hatfield 24/4/35.
Bradford 31/1/42.
Hatfield 15/10/43.
Annesley 4/11/51.
Ardsley 16/5/54.
Copley Hill 3/10/54.
Plaistow 18/12/55.
Tilbury 17/9/56.
Stratford 31/8/58.

Where there were two sunken footsteps, placing the number between them could give the impression of slight reduction of the height of the figures. No.69692 was ex-works 29th September 1948 and had been fitted with a smokebox numberplate.

This style was still in use when 69655 was ex-works on 13th August 1949. It was probably the last to be lettered because the emblem was applied from 21st August 1949.

The next change did not affect the number but the careful painting of fifteen letters was eliminated by transfer applied emblem. No.69681 had the emblem when ex-works 24th September 1949.

As passenger tank engines N7 class was entitled to BR red, cream and grey lining but Stratford were less than enthusiastic about applying it. This 7th June 1953 photograph of 69608 shows it ex-works from a general repair still without lining which would be its state then at least to 19th June 1956.

2655 cont./
RENUMBERED:
  9695 7/9/46.
  69695 19/6/48 .

CONDEMNED: 1/12/58.
Cut up at Stratford.

_____

2656

W Beardmore 319.

To traffic 26/8/27.

REPAIRS:
Str. 1/5—20/7/29.**G**.
Str. 19/9—20/11/31.**G**.
Str. 24/1—24/3/34.**G**.
Str. 8/3—15/4/36.**G**.
Str. 29/4—3/6/38.**G**.
Str. 10/8—11/10/40.**G**.
Str. 31/7—12/11/43.**G**.
Str. 30/5—27/7/46.**G**.
Altered to N7/3.
Str. 9/6—24/8/47.**H**.
Str. 28/3—30/4/49.**G**.
Str. 25/10—9/11/51.**N/C**.
Push-pull gear fitted.
Str. 27/8—27/9/52.**G**.
Str. 10/4—14/5/55.**G**.
Str. 16/12/56—2/1/57.**C/L**.
Str. 24/3—24/4/58.**C/L**.
Str. 9/3—17/4/59.**G**.

BOILERS:
  2101.
    980 21/11/31.
  2018 24/3/34.
  2045 15/4/36.
  2113 3/6/38.
  2042 11/10/40.
  2112 12/11/43.
  1906 27/7/46.
  1971 30/4/49.
  1971 reno.29049 9/11/51.
  29081 27/9/52.
  29135 *(new)* 14/5/55.
  29092 17/4/59.

SHEDS:
King's Cross.
Hatfield 9/9/33.
Bradford 8/4/42.
Hatfield 12/11/43.
Norwich 15/3/53.
Ardsley 6/6/54.
Copley Hill 3/10/54.
Bradford 10/7/55.
Copley Hill 1/4/56.
Yarmouth 4/11/56.
Stratford 29/9/57.
Hatfield 25/10/59.
King's Cross 1/1/61.
Stratford 9/4/61.

RENUMBERED:
  9696 27/7/46.
  69696 30/4/49.

CONDEMNED: 27/4/61.
Cut up at Stratford.

_____

2657

W Beardmore 320.

To traffic 31/8/27.

REPAIRS:
Str. 25/3—8/6/29.**G**.
Str. 1/8—26/9/31.**G**.
Str. 7—27/7/33.**L**.
Steam brake off.
Westinghouse brake fitted.
Str. 13/9—2/11/34.**G**.
Str. 8/9—9/10/36.**G**.
Condensing gear removed.
Str. 17—26/11/36.**L**.
Str. 6/7—8/8/38.**G**.
Str. 5/4—11/5/39.**L**.
Str. 7/4—1/6/40.**G**.
Str. 31/10—3/12/42.**G**.
Str. 8—11/12/42.**N/C**.
Str. 18/3—4/5/45.**G**.
Altered to N7/3.
Str. 6/2—24/3/48.**G**.
Str. 11/10—11/11/50.**G**.
Str. 17/6—31/7/53.**G**.
Str. 30/4—16/6/56.**G**.
Str. 6—13/8/58.**C/L**.
Str. 7/10—27/11/59.**G**.

BOILERS:
  2102.
  2051 2/11/34.
  2036 9/10/36.
  2045 8/8/38.
  2049 1/6/40.
  2105 3/12/42.
  1933 4/5/45.
  1925 24/3/48.
  29011 11/11/50.
  29105 31/7/53.
  29039 16/6/56.
  29078 27/11/59.

SHEDS:
King's Cross.
Cambridge 31/3/33.
King's Cross 30/5/33.
Stratford 10/6/33.
Ipswich 29/11/48.
Stratford 14/5/50.

RENUMBERED:
  9697 2/9/46.
  ᴇ9697 24/3/48.
  69697 11/11/50.

CONDEMNED: 16/9/62.
Cut up at Stratford.

_____

2658

W. Beardmore 321.

To traffic 5/9/27.

REPAIRS:
Str. 16/5—27/7/29.**G**.
Str. 25/7—2/10/31.**G**.
Str. 6/4—11/5/34.**G**.
Str. 10/3—16/4/36.**G**.
Str. 9/10—9/11/37.**G**.
Str. 21/10—1/12/39.**G**.
Str. 28/3—6/5/42.**G**.
Str. 16/5—30/6/45.**G**.
Str. 24/3—13/5/48.**G**.
Str. 8—17/8/49.**C/L**.
Push-pull gear fitted.
Str. 7/8—22/9/50.**G**.
Altered to N7/3.
Str. 4/6—3/7/54.**G**.
Str. 2/11—8/12/56.**G**.
Str. 21/9—6/11/59.**G**.

BOILERS:
  2103.
  2100 2/10/31.
  2106 11/5/34.
  2023 16/4/36.
  2088 9/11/37.
  2099 1/12/39.
  2030 6/5/42.
  2032 30/6/45.
  2095 13/5/48.
  29100 22/9/50.
  29146 3/7/54.
  29014 8/12/56.
  29029 6/11/59.

SHEDS:
King's Cross.
Hatfield 9/9/33.
Bradford1 7/5/42.
Hatfield 22/10/43.
Neasden 21/8/49.
King's Cross 15/7/51.
Ardsley 22/7/51.
King's Cross 16/9/51.
Norwich 4/7/54.
Yarmouth 1/7/56.
Tilbury 7/10/56.
King's Lynn 3/3/58.
Hatfield 1/3/59.
King's Cross 1/1/61.
Stratford. 9/4/61.

RENUMBERED:
  9698 7/9/46.
  69698 13/5/48.

CONDEMNED: 10/9/61.
Cut up at Stratford.

_____

2659

W Beardmore 322.

To traffic 10/9/27.

REPAIRS:
Str. 25/7—4/10/29.**G**.
Str. 30/8—31/10/31.**G**.
Str. 2/8—29/9/33.**G**.
Steam brake off.
Westinghouse brake fitted
Str. 13/6—12/7/35.**G**.
Str. 6/1—20/2/37.**G**.
Condensing gear removed
Str. 17/1—23/2/39.**G**.
Str. 18/7—15/8/40.**G**.
Str. 27/3—17/5/41.**G**.
Str. 17—26/2/43.**L**.
Altered to N7/3.
Str. 30/10—10/12/43.**G**.
Str. 16/12/45—12/1/46.**G**.
Str. 27/5—6/7/48.**G**.
Str. 6/4—5/5/51.**G**.
Str. 12/10—7/11/53.**G**.
Str. 21/3—22/4/55.**C/L**.
Str. 20/11—15/12/56.**G**.
Str. 19/10—21/11/57.**C/L**.
Str. 11—21/8/58.**C/L**.
Str. 29/2—31/3/60.**C/L**.
Str. 7—22/4/60.**N/C**.

BOILERS:
  2105.
  2089 29/9/33.
  2121 12/7/35.
  2101 20/2/37.
  2037 23/2/39.
  2119 15/8/40.
  1976 10/12/43.
  1979 12/1/46.
  1927 6/7/48.
  29029 5/5/51.
  29036 7/11/53.
  29018 15/12/56.

SHEDS:
Hatfield.
King's Cross 15/1/28.
Hatfield 23/1/29.
Stratford 29/9/33.
Ipswich 29/11/48.
Stratford 14/5/50.

RENUMBERED:
  9699 2/9/46.
  69699 3/7/48.

CONDEMNED: 24/11/60.
Cut up at Stratford.

_____

No.69691, ex-works 13th October 1950, provides first evidence so far established of N7 with BR lining. Note the number displayed on the rear buffer beam, the only one so noted.

Application of lining did become general but the standard of cleaning varied from almost perfect to nil.

Enfield was a Stratford sub-shed which maintained a pride in its engines and kept them in immaculate condition. Note polished steel ring o

ebox door and all brass details given attention.

2660

W. Beardmore 323.

To traffic 16/9/27.

REPAIRS:
Str. 3/7—26/9/29.**G.**
Str. 1/1—4/3/32.**G.**
Str. 7/6—5/7/33.**L.**
Steam brake removed.
Westinghouse brake fitted.
Str. 1/11—6/12/34.**G.**
Str. 13/6—24/7/36.**G.**
Condensing gear removed.
Str. 2/1—3/2/38.**G.**
Str. 13/1—17/2/40.**G.**
Str. 13/6—26/8/42.**L/I.**
Str. 19/10—21/12/44.**G.**
Str. 3/10—12/11/47.**G.**
Str. 3/12/50—6/1/51.**G.**
Altered to N7/3.
Str. 16/2—2/4/53.**G.**
Str. 24/4—6/5/53.**N/C.**
Str. 3—17/1/56.**C/L.**
Str. 17/5—28/6/56.**G.**
Str. 20/5—19/6/59.**G.**
Str. 2/5—3/6/60.**C/L.**

BOILERS:
2104.
2115 4/3/32.
2005 6/12/34.
2119 24/7/36.
 981 3/2/38.
2088 17/2/40.
2006 21/12/44.
2036 12/11/47.
29108 6/1/51.
29003 2/4/53.
29049 28/6/56.
29020 19/6/59.

SHEDS:
Hatfield.
King's Cross 13/1/28.
Cambridge 30/3/33.
King's Cross 31/5/33.
Stratford 7/6/33.
Ipswich 17/10/48.
Stratford 14/5/50.

RENUMBERED:
 9700 29/8/46.
69700 6/1/51.

CONDEMNED: 4/12/60.
Cut up at Stratford.

2661

W. Beardmore 324.

To traffic 24/9/27.

REPAIRS:
Str. 6/7—28/9/29.**G.**
Str. 17/10—18/12/31.**G.**
Str. 7/6—6/7/33.**L.**
Steam brake off.
Westinghouse brake fitted.
Str. 2/9—15/11/34.**G.**
Str. 19/8—14/9/36.**G.**
Condensing gear removed.
Str. 26/6—3/8/38.**G.**
Str. 31/5—2/7/40.**G.**
Str. 13/6—28/7/42.**H.**
Str. 23/1—16/3/43.**G.**
Str. 5/11—9/12/44.**G.**
Str. 20/8—4/10/47.**G.**
Altered to N7/3.
Str. 21/5—24/6/50.**G.**
Str. 23/12—6/2/53.**G.**
Str. 12—20/2/53.**N/C.**
Str. 16/6—30/7/54.**C/L.**
Str. 24/11/55—13/1/56.**G.**
Str. 2/9—3/10/58.**G.**
Str. 2/5—10/6/60.**C/L.**

BOILERS:
2106.
2098 18/12/31.
 982 15/11/34.
2054 14/9/36.
2035 3/8/38.
2105 2/7/40.
2021 28/7/42.
1969 4/10/47.
1990 24/6/50.
29087 6/2/53.
29089 13/1/56.
29017 3/10/58.

SHEDS:
Hatfield.
King's Cross 15/6/28.
Cambridge 29/3/33.
King's Cross 1/6/33.
Stratford 7/6/33.
Ipswich 17/10/48.
Stratford 14/5/50.
Colchester 16/7/50.
Stratford 8/7/51.

RENUMBERED:
 9701 1/9/46.
69701 24/6/50.

CONDEMNED: 4/12/60.
Cut up at Stratford.

2600

Doncaster 1669.

To traffic 19/11/27.

REPAIRS:
Don. 12/12/27—14/1/28.**L.**
Str. 2/5—20/6/30.**G.**
Str. 6/2—17/3/33.**G.**
Str. 10/5—26/6/35.**G.**
Str. 3/4—26/5/37.**G.**
Condensing gear removed.
Str. 30/3—19/5/39.**G.**
Str. 6—9/6/39.**L.**
Str. 10/5—16/6/41.**G.**
Str. 25/9—5/11/43.**G.**
Str. 20/1—20/2/46.**G.**
Str. 5/9—19/11/48.**G.**
Str. 19/10—24/11/51.**G.**
Str. 10/2—5/3/54.**C/L.**
Str. 12/8—4/9/54.**G.**
Str. 3/7—2/8/56.**C/L.**
Str. 27/11—8/12/56.**N/C.**
Str. 24/4—17/5/57.**C/L.**
Str. 5—21/6/57.**C/L.**
Str. 13/3—18/4/58.**G.**

BOILERS:
2055.
2065 17/3/33.
2055 26/6/35.
2079 26/5/37.
2057 19/5/39.
1958 16/6/41.
1974 5/11/43.
1948 20/2/46.
29050 24/11/51.
29013 4/9/54.
29113 18/4/58.

SHEDS:
Ardsley.
Stratford 4/2/28.

RENUMBERED:
 9702 7/9/46.
69702 13/11/48.

CONDEMNED: 17/3/61.
Cut up at Stratford.

_____

2601

Doncaster 1670.

To traffic 5/11/27.

REPAIRS:
Str. 7/1—12/3/30.**G.**

Str. 11/6—26/7/32.**G.**
Str. 7/12/34—29/1/35.**G.**
Str. 11/11—16/12/36.**G.**
Condensing gear removed.
Str. 18/9—27/10/38.**G.**
Str. 11/6—11/8/39.**G.**
Str. 20/10—4/12/40.**G.**
Str. 8/4—26/6/43.**G.**
Str. 6/5—2/6/45.**G.**
Str. 22/11—13/12/45.**L.**
Str. 27/3—27/5/47.**G.**
Str. 23/3—5/4/48.**L.**
Str. 4/2—2/4/49.**G.**
Str. 4—6/4/49.**N/C.**
Str. 25/10—26/11/49.**G.**
Str. 29/8—23/10/52.**G.**
Str. 29/4—14/5/54.**C/L.**
Str. 2/8—10/9/55.**G.**
Str. 10/1—2/3/56.**C/L.**

BOILERS:
2056.
2060 26/7/32.
2072 29/1/35.
2056 16/12/36.
1953 27/10/38.
2071 11/8/39.
2074 4/12/40.
2070 26/6/43.
1935 2/6/45.
2060 26/11/49.
29035 23/10/52.
29052 10/9/55.

SHEDS:
Stratford.
Ipswich 20/8/50.
Stratford 7/1/51.

RENUMBERED:
 9703 7/9/46.
69703 3/4/48.

CONDEMNED: 1/1/59.
Cut up at Stratford.

_____

2602

Doncaster 1671.

To traffic 10/11/27.

REPAIRS:
Don. 3/12/27—11/1/28.**L.**
Str. 1/3—17/4/30.**G.**
Str. 7/7—18/8/32.**G.**
Str. 16/7—21/8/34.**G.**
Str. 24/5—25/6/36.**G.**
Condensing gear removed.
Str. 13/2—18/3/38.**G.**

2602 cont./
Str. 18/6—24/8/39.**H.**
Str. 13/3—26/4/40.**G.**
Str. 21/1—24/2/42.**G.**
Str. 9—27/3/43.**L.**
Str. 13/1—18/3/44.**G.**
Str. 2/6—1/8/46.**G.**
Str. 27/2—30/3/49.**G.**
Str. 9/2—1/4/50.**C/L.**
Str. 26/11/51—12/1/52.**G.**
Str. 11/3—16/4/55.**G.**
Str. 19/9—1/10/55.**N/C.**
Str. 18—30/11/56.**N/C.**
Str. 18/8—19/9/58.**G.**

BOILERS:
 2057.
 2056 18/8/32.
 1950 21/8/34.
 1952 25/6/36.
 2083 18/3/38.
 2062 24/8/39.
 2069 24/2/42.
 1983 18/3/44.
 1957 1/8/46.
 1909 30/3/49.
29052 12/1/52.
29098 *(new)* 16/4/55.
29041 19/9/58.

SHEDS:
Ardsley.
Stratford 6/2/28.
Hatfield 14/9/52.
Stratford 24/1/60.

RENUMBERED:
 9704 26/7/46.
 69704 26/3/49.

CONDEMNED: 18/10/60.
Cut up at Stratford.

_____

2603

Doncaster 1672.

To traffic 12/11/27.

REPAIRS:
Str. 3/5—3/7/30.**G.**
Str. 14/7—30/8/32.**G.**
Str. 24/3—26/6/34.**G.**
Str. 30/5—6/7/36.**G.**
Condensing gear removed.
Str. 20/1—25/2/38.**G.**
Str. 1/1—2/2/40.**G.**
Str. 21/4—28/5/42.**H.**
Str. 6—10/6/42.**L.**
Str. 20/8—23/9/44.**G.**
Str. 5/5—22/6/46.**G.**
Str. 9/6—5/7/48.**L.**
Str. 12/6—23/7/49.**G.**
Str. 17/6—9/8/52.**G.**

Str. 2—6/2/54.**C/L.**
Str. 10/10—8/2/56.**C/L.**
Str. 14/8—29/9/56.**G.**
Str. 18/6/59. *Not repaired.*

BOILERS:
 2058.
 2057 30/8/32.
 2059 26/6/34.
 1954 6/7/36.
 2068 25/2/38.
 2081 2/2/40.
 2062 28/5/42.
 1956 23/9/44.
 1973 22/6/46.
 1906 23/7/49.
29074 9/8/52.
29093 29/9/56.

SHEDS:
Ardsley.
Stratford 12/12/27.

RENUMBERED:
 9705 27/10/46.
 69705 3/7/48.

CONDEMNED: 22/6/59.
Cut up at Stratford.

_____

2604

Doncaster 1673.

To traffic 19/11/27.

REPAIRS:
Str. 22/2—12/4/30.**G.**
Str. 2/4—13/5/32.**G.**
Str. 26/6—27/7/34.**G.**
Str. 16/5—26/6/36.**G.**
Condensing gear removed.
Str. 15/1—25/2/38.**G.**
Str. 3/2—9/3/40.**G.**
Str. 23/6—4/9/42.**G.**
Str. 28/1—28/2/45.**G.**
Str. 23/11/47—2/1/48.**G.**
Str. 3/5—8/6/48.**H.**
Str. 21/4—21/5/49.**C/L.**
Str. 25/6—19/8/50.**G.**
Str. 12/9—10/10/53.**G.**
Str. 9/12/56—12/1/57.**G.**
Str. 18/1—12/2/60.**N/C.**
Str. 16—23/6/60.**C/L.**

BOILERS:
 2059.
 1950 13/5/32.
 2057 27/7/34.
 2084 26/6/36.
 2061 25/2/38.
 2065 9/3/40.
 2076 4/9/42.
 2058 28/2/45.

1919 2/1/48.
1933 8/6/48.
1994 19/8/50.
29107 10/10/53.
29015 12/1/57.

SHEDS:
Ardsley.
Stratford 19/1/28.
Norwich 27/3/49.
Lowestoft 22/7/56.
Norwich 23/9/56.
Lowestoft 2/6/57.
Stratford 6/9/59.

RENUMBERED:
 9706 2/11/46.
 69706 5/6/48.

CONDEMNED: 4/12/60.
Cut up at Stratford.

_____

2605

Doncaster 1674.

To traffic 26/11/27.

REPAIRS:
Str. 2/10—18/12/29.**G.**
Str. 30/4—9/6/32.**G.**
Str. 9/5—29/6/34.**G.**
Str. 3/6—2/7/36.**G.**
Condensing gear removed.
Str. 15/4—23/5/38.**G.**
Str. 30/4—1/6/40.**G.**
Str. 12/12/42—24/2/43.**G.**
Str. 4/3—21/4/45.**G.**
Str. 21/9—18/11/47.**G.**
Str. 7/5—17/6/50.**G.**
Str. 15—25/4/52.**C/L.**
Str. 21/3—18/4/53.**G.**
Str. 9/4—26/5/56.**G.**
Str. 11/7—2/8/57.**C/L.**
Str. 5/11—20/12/57.**C/L.**
Str. 20/8—2/10/59.**G.**

BOILERS:
 2060.
 1951 9/6/32.
 1955 2/7/36.
 2085 23/5/38.
 2068 1/6/40.
 1965 24/2/43.
 1932 21/4/45.
 1915 18/11/47.
 1989 17/6/50.
 1989 reno.29066 25/4/52.
29126 *(new)* 18/4/53.
29087 26/5/56.
29056 2/10/59.

SHEDS:
Ardsley.

Stratford 6/1/28.
Norwich 25/3/49.
Ipswich 20/4/49.
Norwich 6/10/49.
Stratford 4/10/59.

RENUMBERED:
 9707 9/9/46.
 69707 17/6/50.

CONDEMNED: 27/4/61.
Cut up at Stratford.

_____

2606

Doncaster 1675.

To traffic 10/12/27.

REPAIRS:
Str. 3/5—27/6/30.**G.**
Str. 16/1—24/2/33.**G.**
Str. 3/9—10/10/34.**G.**
Str. 19/5—26/6/36.**G.**
Condensing gear removed.
Str. 11/1—18/2/38.**G.**
Str. 17/12/39—22/1/40.**G.**
Str. 27/2—14/3/41.**L.**
Str. 15/5—26/6/42.**G.**
Str. 7—17/9/42.**L.**
Str. 27/10—22/11/44.**G.**
Str. 26/3—19/4/46.**L.**
Str. 26/8—16/10/47.**G.**
Str. 20/7—22/9/48.**L.**
Tablet exchanging
apparatus fitted.
Str. 28/5—1/7/50.**G.**
Str. 10/8—30/9/50.**C/L.**
Str. 2—30/1/54.**G.**
Push-pull gear fitted.
Westinghouse replaced
by steam brake.
Str. 20/10—3/11/56.**C/L.**
Str. 11/4—24/5/57.**G.**
Str. 12—14/5/59.**N/C.**
Str. 31/5—9/8/60.**N/C.**

BOILERS:
 2061.
 2073 24/2/33.
 2056 10/10/34.
 1953 26/6/36.
 2065 18/2/38.
 2058 22/1/40.
 2077 26/6/42.
 2063 22/11/44.
 1936 16/10/47.
 1962 1/7/50.
 1962 reno.29005 30/9/50.
29112 30/1/54.
29100 24/5/57.

SHEDS:
Ardsley.

Further change took place from 5th April 1957 when 69674 was ex-works with the BR crest instead of the emblem. The crest was applied by transfer.

On the right hand side the crest had the lion facing forward, i.e. to the right, which in heraldry was a serious mistake. This went on for more than a year, 69692 being ex-works 18th April 1958.

In their later days (this is a March 1961 photograph), some carried electrification warning signs on the tank and bunker. 69632 got the wrong crest ex-works 2nd August 1957 and this was worn until its 16th September 1962 withdrawal, despite a casual/heavy repair which took from 25th April to 12th August 1960.

2606 cont./
Stratford 31/1/28.
Ipswich 7/10/48.
Melton Constable 5/12/48.
Norwich 30/7/50.
Melton Constable 3/12/50.
Norwich 14/10/51.
Yarmouth 14/3/54.
Stratford 3/10/54.
Yarmouth 14/11/54.
Lowestoft 7/7/57.
Yarmouth 29/9/57.
Stratford 1/2/59.
Parkeston 24/1/60.
Stratford 1/1/61.

RENUMBERED:
   9708 2/11/46.
   69708 18/9/48.

CONDEMNED: 13/1/61.
Cut up at Stratford.

_____

2607

Doncaster 1676.

To traffic 15/12/27.

REPAIRS:
Str. 10/5—30/7/30.**G.**
Str. 28/10—6/12/32.**G.**
Str. 13/8—5/10/34.**G.**
Str. 16—20/9/35.**L.**
Str. 6/9—1/10/36.**G.**
Condensing gear removed.
Str. 5/3—8/4/38.**G.**
Str. 12/4—21/5/40.**G.**
Str. 9/12—1/3/43.**G.**
Str. 23/5—25/6/43.**L.**
Str. 13/5—22/6/45.**G.**
Str. 11—29/12/45.**L.**
Str. 2/6—13/8/48.**G.**
Str. 22/4—15/6/51.**G.**
Str. 28—29/6/51.**N/C.**
Str. 17/2—26/3/54.**G.**
Str. 22/12/54—11/3/55.**C/L.**
Str. 23/9—4/10/56.**N/C.**
Str. 3/2—7/3/58.**G.**
Str. 5—29/1/60.**C/L.**

BOILERS:
   2062.
   2067 6/12/32.
   2058 5/10/34.
   2086 1/10/36.
   1954 8/4/38.
   2083 21/5/40.
   1966 1/3/43.
   1938 22/6/45.
   1929 13/8/48.
   29031 15/6/51.
   29045 26/3/54.
   29038 7/3/58.

SHEDS:
Ardsley.
Stratford 1/3/28.
Norwich 19/3/49.
Hatfield 3/5/53.
Colchester 30/6/57.
Stratford 29/9/57.

RENUMBERED:
   9709 28/11/46.
   69709 13/8/48.

CONDEMNED: 1/11/60.
Cut up at Stratford.

_____

2608

Doncaster 1677.

To traffic 13/12/27.

REPAIRS:
Str. 24/8—30/10/29.**G.**
Str. 16/1—26/3/32.**G.**
Str. 10/2—23/3/34.**G.**
Str. 19/10—25/11/35.**G.**
Str. 26/7—1/9/37.**G.**
Condensing gear removed.
Str. 28/5—10/7/39.**G.**
Str. 11/12/41—24/1/42.**G.**
Str. 18/2—25/3/44.**G.**
Str. 30/3—5/6/47.**G.**
Str. 6—17/12/48.**L.**
Str. 16/10—12/11/49.**G.**
Str. 18—23/11/49.**N/C.**
Str. 27/10—29/11/52.**G.**
Str. 4—22/10/54.**C/L.**
Str. 1/6—28/7/56.**G.**
Str. 4—14/5/59.**L/I.**
Str. 21/12/59—12/2/60.**L/I.**

BOILERS:
   2063.
   2082 23/3/34.
   2085 25/11/35.
   2077 1/9/37.
   2078 10/7/39.
   2073 24/1/42.
   1984 25/3/44.
   1943 12/11/49.
   29084 29/11/52.
   29085 28/7/56.

SHEDS:
Ardsley.
Stratford 14/1/28.
Ipswich 22/5/49.
Stratford 29/5/49.

RENUMBERED:
   9710 9/9/46.
   69710 11/12/48.

CONDEMNED: 10/9/61.
Cut up at Stratford.

_____

2609

Doncaster 1678.

To traffic 21/12/27.

REPAIRS:
Str. 15/3—9/5/30.**G.**
Str. 6/6—15/7/32.**G.**
Str. 10/2—16/3/34.**G.**
Str. 9—22/6/35.**L.**
Str. 26/2—26/3/36.**G.**
Str. 30/11—31/12/37.**G.**
Condensing gear removed.
Str. 20/9—7/11/39.**G.**
Str. 11/1—13/2/42.**G.**
Str. 11/6—24/7/44.**G.**
Str. 25/2—14/4/47.**G.**
Str. 3/11—3/12/49.**G.**
Str. 30/3—8/5/53.**G.**
Str. 21/3—1/4/55.**C/L.**
Str. 19/4—9/5/56.**C/L.**
Str. 15/11—29/12/56.**G.**
Str. 31/7—30/8/57.**C/L.**
Str. 27/10—5/11/58.**C/L.**

BOILERS:
   2064.
   2059 15/7/32.
   2086 16/3/34.
   2082 26/3/36.
   2074 31/12/37.
   2076 7/11/39.
   2060 13/2/42.
   1914 14/4/47.
   1981 3/12/49.
   29127 *(new)* 8/5/53.
   29103 29/12/56.

SHEDS:
Ardsley.
Stratford 30/1/28.
Ipswich 22/5/49.
Stratford 29/5/49.
Colchester 4/6/50.
Stratford 16/7/50.
Ipswich 20/8/50.
Stratford 24/9/50.
King's Lynn 8/10/50.
Stratford 29/10/50.

RENUMBERED:
   9711 6/9/46.
   69711 3/12/49.

CONDEMNED: 23/11/59.
Cut up at Stratford.

_____

2610

Doncaster 1679.

To traffic 2/1/28.

REPAIRS:
Str. 28/6—18/9/30.**G.**
Str. 10/1—27/2/33.**G.**
Str. 16/1—23/3/35.**G.**
Str. 4/3—16/4/37.**G.**
Condensing gear removed
Str. 18/2—31/3/39.**G.**
Str. 12/4—5/6/41.**G.**
Str. 5/12/43—21/1/44.**G.**
Str. 6/5—13/6/46.**G.**
Str. 29/12/48—15/2/49.**G.**
Str. 8/11—22/12/51.**G.**
Str. 11/3—2/4/53.**C/L.**
Str. 24/1—5/3/55.**G.**
Str. 3/11—2/12/55.**C/L.**
Str. 24/4—30/5/58.**G.**
Str. 30/3—6/5/60.**C/L.**

BOILERS:
   2065.
   2078 27/2/33.
   2074 23/3/35.
   2063 16/4/37.
   2067 31/3/39.
   1957 5/6/41.
   2071 21/1/44.
   2074 13/6/46.
   2078 15/2/49.
   29043 22/12/51.
   29095 *(new)* 5/3/55.
   24800 30/5/58.

SHEDS:
Ardsley.
Stratford 1/3/28.
Boston 2/12/49.
Stratford 23/4/50.
King's Lynn 8/10/50.
Stratford 29/10/50.

RENUMBERED:
   9712 27/10/46.
   69712 12/2/49.

CONDEMNED: 4/12/60.
Cut up at Stratford.

_____

2611

Doncaster 1680.

To traffic 14/1/28.

REPAIRS:
Str. 2/5—20/6/30.**G.**
Str. 21/8—13/10/32.**G.**
Str. 1/11—28/12/34.**G.**

The longest serving N7 was No.999ᴇ, to traffic 19th March 1924; 7999 from 31st March 1926 then 9621 from 2nd January 1947 and finally

8th January 1949 to withdrawal on 11th September 1962. It was ex-works as shown on 11th March 1960, its last general repair.

After withdrawal, 69621 was bought for preservation by Dr. R.F.Youell, and until September 1973 was stored in Leeds Neville Hill shed and

to the Stour Valley line at Chappel & Wakes Colne.

2611 cont./
Str. 29/12/36—30/1/37.**G.**
Condensing gear removed.
Str. 11/9—25/10/38.**G.**
Str. 26/6—10/8/40.**G.**
Str. 27—28/5/42.**L.**
Str. 20/9—30/10/42.**H/I.**
Str. 24/2—3/3/43.**L.**
Str. 7/1—2/2/45.**G.**
Str. 9/2—19/3/47.**G.**
Str. 27/3—12/4/48.**L.**
Str. 9—29/10/49.**G.**
Str. 23/6—27/8/52.**G.**
Str. 7/9—26/10/55.**G.**
Str. 14/3—21/7/56.**C/L.**
Str. 17—25/9/56.**C/L.**
Str. 13/6—26/7/57.**C/L.**
Str. 27/4—30/5/59.**G.**
Str. 30/6—29/7/60.**C/L.**

BOILERS:
2066.
2064 13/10/32.
2067 30/1/37.
2082 25/10/38.
1953 10/8/40.
2058 30/10/42.
2077 2/2/45.
1981 19/3/47.
1907 29/10/49.
29118 *(new)* 27/8/52.
29088 26/10/55.
29108 30/5/59.

SHEDS:
Ardsley.
Stratford 25/2/28.

RENUMBERED:
9713 10/9/46.
69713 10/4/48.

CONDEMNED: 10/9/61.
Cut up at Stratford.
_____

2612

Doncaster 1681.

To traffic 27/1/28.

REPAIRS:
Str. 24/5—21/8/30.**G.**
Str. 20/10—25/11/32.**G.**
Str. 8/1—16/3/35.**G.**
Str. 2/3—9/4/37.**G.**
Condensing gear removed.
Str. 19/3—29/4/39.**G.**
Str. 14/6—29/7/41.**G.**
Str. 3/2—20/3/42.**L.**
Str. 11/3—15/4/44.**G.**
Str. 1/9—5/10/44.**G.**
Str. 9/6—15/8/46.**G.**
Str. 19—24/8/46.**N/C.**

Str. 25/8—1/10/49.**G.**
Str. 13—14/10/49.**N/C.**
Str. 14/6—26/8/50.**C/H.**
Str. 9/12/52—17/1/53.**G.**
Str. 14—22/6/54.**C/L.**
Str. 1/11—10/12/55.**G.**
Str. 8/3—14/4/56.**C/L.**
Str. 6—21/6/57.**C/L.**
Str. 25—29/8/58.**C/L.**
Str. 9/9—23/10/59.**G.**

BOILERS:
2067.
2074 25/11/32.
2080 16/3/35.
2078 9/4/37.
1956 29/4/39.
1961 29/7/41.
1959 15/4/44.
2062 5/10/44.
1908 15/8/46.
1910 1/10/49.
29120 *(new)* 17/1/53.
29078 10/12/55.
29026 23/10/59.

SHEDS:
Ardsley.
Stratford 5/3/28.

RENUMBERED:
9714 27/10/46.
69714 1/10/49.

CONDEMNED: 10/9/61.
Cut up at Stratford.
_____

2613

Doncaster 1682.

To traffic 28/1/28.

REPAIRS:
Str. 5/7—25/9/30.**G.**
Str. 13/10—15/11/32.**G.**
Str. 18/12/34—27/2/35.**G.**
Str. 28/2—9/4/37.**G.**
Condensing gear removed.
Str. 6/3—15/4/39.**G.**
Str. 17/7—12/8/40.**L.**
Str. 30/5—2/8/41.**G.**
Str. 4/8—12/10/43.**G.**
Str. 5/8—8/9/45.**G.**
Str. 15/8—15/9/48.**G.**
Str. 3/10—17/11/51.**G.**
Str. 26/5—25/6/54.**G.**
Str. 2/12/54—15/1/55.**G.**
Str. 16/3—22/4/55.**C/L.**
Str. 24/11—23/12/55.**C/L.**
Str. 28/5—28/6/58.**G.**
Str. 21—29/7/58.**N/C.**
Str. 8—24/12/59.**C/L.**

BOILERS:
2068.
2070 15/11/32.
2060 27/2/35.
2073 9/4/37.
2059 15/4/39.
1960 2/8/41.
1972 12/10/43.
1941 8/9/45.
1912 15/9/48.
1912 reno.29047 17/11/51.
29041 15/1/55.
29095 28/6/58.

SHEDS:
Ardsley.
Stratford 28/4/28.

RENUMBERED:
9715 11/11/46.
69715 11/9/48.

CONDEMNED: 4/12/60.
Cut up at Stratford.
_____

2614

Doncaster 1683.

To traffic 4/2/28.

REPAIRS:
Str. 26/7—17/10/30.**G.**
Str. 21/7—8/9/32.**G.**
Str. 13/5—18/7/34.**G.**
Str. 2/7—8/8/36.**G.**
Condensing gear removed.
Str. 21/4—17/5/38.**G.**
Str. 26/5—29/6/40.**G.**
Str. 8/12/42—5/3/43.**G.**
Str. 17/6—24/8/45.**G.**
Str. 3/3/48.**L.**
Str. 12/7—1/9/48.**G.**
Str. 16/8—15/9/51.**G.**
Str. 18/1—12/2/55.**G.**
Str. 5—15/10/56.**C/L.**
Str. 5—27/6/57.**C/L.**

BOILERS:
2069.
2058 8/9/32.
2063 18/7/34.
1950 8/8/36.
2075 17/5/38.
2070 29/6/40.
2081 5/3/43.
1982 24/8/45.
1944 1/9/48.
29040 15/9/51.
29134 *(new)* 12/2/55.

SHEDS:
Ardsley.
Stratford 13/4/28.

Boston 2/12/49.
Stratford 14/5/50.
King's Lynn 8/10/50.
Stratford 29/10/50.
Colchester 6/7/52.
Stratford 22/9/52.

RENUMBERED:
9716 26/10/46.
69716 28/8/48.

CONDEMNED: 12/2/59.
Cut up at Stratford.
_____

2615

Doncaster 1684.

To traffic 17/2/28.

REPAIRS:
Str. 23/8—24/10/30.**G.**
Str. 12/12/32—20/1/33.**G.**
Str. 19/1—4/4/35.**G.**
Str. 25/1—4/3/37.**G.**
Condensing gear removed.
Str. 27/5—5/6/37.**L.**
Str. 23/10—6/12/38.**G.**
Str. 14/9—31/10/40.**G.**
Str. 6/6—26/8/43.**G.**
Str. 8/5—2/6/45.**G.**
Str. 16/12/47—17/1/48.**G.**
Str. 2/7—6/8/49.**C/H.**
Str. 1/8—2/9/50.**G.**
Str. 21/4—16/5/53.**G.**
Str. 11—27/1/56.**C/L.**
Str. 29/10—1/12/56.**G.**

BOILERS:
2071.
2062 20/1/33.
2069 4/4/35.
1951 4/3/37.
2056 6/12/38.
2082 31/10/40.
1967 26/8/43.
1937 2/6/45.
1923 17/1/48.
1936 2/9/50.
29066 16/5/53.
29131 1/12/56.

SHEDS:
Ardsley.
Stratford 28/3/28.
Ipswich 29/5/49.
Stratford 14/5/50.
Colchester 1/7/51.
Stratford 23/9/51.
Colchester 11/11/51.
Stratford 22/9/52.

2615 cont./
RENUMBERED:
 9717 3/11/46.
 E**9717** 17/1/48.
 69717 6/8/49.

CONDEMNED: 1/1/59.
Cut up at Stratford.

_____

2616

Doncaster 1685.

To traffic 27/2/28.

REPAIRS:
Str. 7/6—21/8/30.**G.**
Str. 24/9—25/10/32.**G.**
Str. 11/1—7/3/35.**G.**
Str. 4/4—22/5/37.**G.**
Condensing gear removed.
Str. 4/4—18/5/39.**G.**
Str. 14/3—11/4/41.**G.**
Str. 5/2—3/4/43.**G.**
Str. 13/2—24/3/44.**G.**
Str. 29/12/46—10/2/47.**G.**
Str. 2/10—5/11/49.**G.**
Str. 30/4—16/5/52.**C/L.**
Str. 10/12/52—30/1/53.**G.**
Str. 5—20/2/53.**N/C.**
Str. 23/2—24/3/53.**N/C.**
Str. 20/10—18/12/54.**C/L.**
Str. 13/10—8/11/55.**C/L.**
Str. 7/1—8/2/57.**G.**
Str. 18/3—22/4/60.**C/L.**

BOILERS:
 2070.
 2069 25/10/32.
 2070 7/3/35.
 2062 22/5/37.
 1951 18/5/39.
 1950 11/4/41.
 2069 24/3/44.
 1983 10/2/47.
 1960 5/11/49.
 1960 reno.29068 16/5/52.
 29086 30/1/53.
 29074 8/2/57.

SHEDS:
Ardsley.
Stratford 21/3/28.
King's Lynn 26/7/59.
Stratford 9/8/59.

RENUMBERED:
 9718 3/11/46.
 69718 5/11/49.

CONDEMNED: 4/12/60.
Cut up at Stratford.

_____

2617

Doncaster 1686.

To traffic 19/3/28.

REPAIRS:
Str. 9/8—16/10/30.**G.**
Str. 12/7—15/9/32.**G.**
Str. 20/9—11/12/34.**G.**
Str. 29/11/36—8/1/37.**G.**
Condensing gear removed.
Str. 25/10—14/12/38.**G.**
Str. 7/12/40—18/1/41.**G.**
Str. 2/6—8/9/43.**G.**
Str. 10—22/9/44.**L.**
Str. 9/12/45—5/1/46.**G.**
Str. 16/9—2/11/48.**G.**
Str. 31/3—5/5/49.**C/L.**
Str. 23/5—11/7/50.**C/H.**
Str. 3/3—10/4/52.**G.**
Str. 22/9—10/10/53.**C/L.**
Str. 21/3—23/4/55.**G.**
Str. 25/9—5/10/56.**N/C.**
Str. 13/8—13/9/57.**C/L.**
Str. 19/5—24/6/58.**C/L.**
Str. 11/5—12/6/59.**G.**

BOILERS:
 2072.
 2066 11/12/34.
 1956 8/1/37.
 2086 14/12/38.
 2084 18/1/41.
 1968 8/9/43.
 1977 5/1/46.
 2082 2/11/48.
 1915 11/7/50.
 29062 10/4/52.
 29032 23/4/55.
 29053 12/6/59.

SHEDS:
Ardsley.
Stratford 13/4/28.
Ipswich 29/5/49.
Stratford 14/5/50.
Colchester 6/7/52.
Stratford 22/9/52.
Colchester 26/10/52.
Stratford 15/11/53.

RENUMBERED:
 9719 10/11/46.
 69719 30/10/48.

CONDEMNED: 24/11/60.
Cut up at Stratford.

_____

2618

Doncaster 1687.

To traffic 14/4/28.

REPAIRS:
Str. 2/8—10/10/30.**G.**
Str. 5/1—16/2/33.**G.**
Str. 19/3—23/5/35.**G.**
Str. 22/8—2/9/36.**L.**
Str. 23/5—25/6/37.**G.**
Condensing gear removed.
Str. 28/5—12/7/39.**G.**
Str. 23/1—8/2/41.**L.**
Str. 25/10—28/11/41.**G.**
Str. 4/6—1/7/44.**G.**
Str. 25/5—14/7/47.**G.**
Str. 8/11—10/12/49.**G.**
Str. 14/4—21/5/52.**G.**
Str. 7/3—9/4/55.**G.**
Str. 10—21/12/56.**C/L.**
Str. 1—30/4/57.**C/L.**
Str. 18/6—1/8/58.**G.**
Str. 7—28/8/59.**C/L.**
Str. 7—22/1/60.**N/C.**

BOILERS:
 2073.
 2077 16/2/33.
 2071 23/5/35.
 2066 25/6/37.
 2080 12/7/39.
 2057 28/11/41.
 1962 1/7/44.
 1952 14/7/47.
 1984 10/12/49.
 29065 21/5/52.
 29040 9/4/55.
 29001 1/8/58.

SHEDS:
Ardsley.
Stratford 18/5/28.
Colchester 8/7/51.
Stratford 6/2/55.
Colchester 24/4/55.
Stratford 16/9/56.

RENUMBERED:
 9720 16/9/46.
 69720 10/12/49.

CONDEMNED: 1/11/60.
Cut up at Stratford.

_____

2619

Doncaster 1688.

To traffic 13/6/28.

REPAIRS:
Str. 16/8—24/10/30.**G.**

Str. 6/10—2/11/32.**G.**
Str. 11/9—30/11/34.**G.**
Str. 6/12/36—14/1/37.**G.**
Condensing gear removed.
Str. 19/1—24/2/39.**G.**
Str. 30/12/40—15/2/41.**G.**
Str. 16/8—22/10/43.**G.**
Str. 24/2—28/3/46.**G.**
Str. 3—25/6/46.**L.**
Str. 14/2—18/3/49.**G.**
Str. 24/5—28/7/51.**G.**
Str. 9—10/6/52.**C/L.**
Str. 12/1—12/2/54.**G.**
Str. 13/10—20/11/54.**C/L.**
Str. 16/3—22/4/55.**C/L.**
Str. 17/10—3/11/55.**N/C.**
Str. 8/3—5/5/56.**C/L.**
Str. 8/1—8/2/58.**G.**
Str. 22/4—27/5/60.**C/L.**

BOILERS:
 2074.
 2066 2/11/32.
 2067 30/11/34.
 2072 14/1/37.
 1955 24/2/39.
 1954 15/2/41.
 1973 22/10/43.
 1953 28/3/46.
 1919 18/3/49.
 29033 28/7/51.
 29037 12/2/54.
 29125 8/2/58.

SHEDS:
Ardsley.
Stratford 25/7/28.
Parkeston 28/10/56.
Colchester 3/2/57.
Stratford 29/9/57.

RENUMBERED:
 9721 25/10/46.
 69721 18/3/49.

CONDEMNED: 4/12/60.
Cut up at Stratford.

_____

2620

Doncaster 1689.

To traffic 30/6/28.

REPAIRS:
Str. 13/9—28/11/30.**G.**
Str. 13/3—28/4/33.**G.**
Str. 21/3—1/5/35.**G.**
Str. 25/8—7/9/36.**L.**
Str. 12/3—8/5/37.**G.**
Condensing gear removed.
Str. 12/2—21/3/39.**G.**
Str. 22/12/40—11/2/41.**G.**
Str. 20/6—7/8/41.**H.**

2620 cont./
Str. 28/8—5/9/42.**L.**
Str. 14/7—21/9/43.**G.**
Str. 30/12—26/1/46.**G.**
Str. 20/12—6/2/49.**G.**
Str. 16—20/2/49.**N/C.**
Str. 7/1—2/2/52.**G.**
Str. 21/3—30/4/55.**G.**
Str. 26/11—6/12/56.**N/C.**
Str. 29/5—14/6/57.**C/L.**
Str. 12/5—13/6/58.**G.**
Str. 9/5—17/6/60.**C/L.**

BOILERS:
2076.
2079 28/4/33.
2062 1/5/35.
2060 8/5/37.
1950 21/3/39.
1952 11/2/41.
2067 7/8/41.
1970 21/9/43.
1971 26/1/46.
1977 6/2/49.
29055 2/2/52.
29034 30/4/55.
29065 13/6/58.

SHEDS:
Ardsley.
Stratford 13/8/28.

RENUMBERED:
9722 8/10/46.
69722 5/2/49.

CONDEMNED: 4/12/60.
Cut up at Stratford.

_____

2621

Doncaster 1690.

To traffic 7/7/28.

REPAIRS:
Str. 30/8—7/11/30.**G.**
Str. 3/11—9/12/32.**G.**
Str. 4/6—25/7/35.**G.**
Str. 27/7—1/9/37.**G.**
Condensing gear removed.
Str. 23/10—4/12/39.**G.**
Str. 14/12/41—29/1/42.**G.**
Str. 7—30/10/43.**L.**
Str. 12/7—7/9/44.**G.**
Str. 22/9—31/10/46.**G.**
Str. 8—15/3/48.**L.**
Str. 15/6—11/8/49.**G.**
Str. 30/9—1/10/49.**N/C.**
Str. 6—29/6/51.**C/L.**
Str. 13/8—6/9/51.**C/L.**
Str. 22/8—1/10/52.**G.**
Str. 1/12/55—21/1/56.**G.**
Str. 12/2—2/3/57.**C/L.**

Str. 20—30/10/58.**C/L.**
Str. 2/6—25/7/59.**G.**
Str. 19/1—13/3/61.**N/C.**

BOILERS:
2075.
2068 9/12/32.
2061 25/7/35.
2064 1/9/37.
2077 4/12/39.
2080 29/1/42.
2072 7/9/44.
1960 31/10/46.
1985 11/8/49.
1985 reno.29035 29/6/51.
29016 1/10/52.
29122 21/1/56.
29063 25/7/59.

SHEDS:
Ardsley.
Stratford 13/8/28.

RENUMBERED:
9723 16/11/46.
69723 11/8/49.

CONDEMNED: 10/9/61.
Cut up at Stratford.

_____

2622

Doncaster 1691.

To traffic 24/7/28.

REPAIRS:
Str. 20/9—20/11/30.**G.**
Str. 3/1—7/2/33.**G.**
Str. 24/1—5/4/35.**G.**
Str. 12/6—1/7/36.**L.**
Str. 30/1—12/3/37.**G.**
Condensing gear removed.
Str. 11/10—14/11/38.**G.**
Str. 10/11—14/12/40.**G.**
Str. 22/11—5/12/42.**L.**
Str. 7/7—10/9/43.**G.**
Str. 29/7—6/9/45.**G.**
Str. 14/8—10/9/49.**G.**
Str. 5/5—12/6/52.**G.**
Str. 23—25/6/52.**N/C.**
Str. 20/8—10/9/53.**C/L.**
Str. 15/4—21/5/55.**C/L.**
Str. 24/10—10/12/55.**G.**
Str. 8—17/10/58.**C/L.**
Str. 13/10—4/12/59.**G.**

BOILERS:
2078.
2071 7/2/33.
2078 5/4/35.
2059 12/3/37.
1952 14/11/38.
2056 14/12/40.

1969 10/9/43.
1940 6/9/45.
1949 10/9/49.
29067 12/6/52.
29060 10/12/55.
29014 4/12/59.

SHEDS:
Ardsley.
Stratford 10/9/28.

RENUMBERED:
9724 2/1/47.
69724 10/9/49.

CONDEMNED: 10/9/61.
Cut up at Stratford.

_____

2623

Doncaster 1692.

To traffic 25/7/28.

REPAIRS:
Str. 18/7—3/10/30.**G.**
Str. 1/2—10/3/33.**G.**
Str. 20/4—5/7/35.**G.**
Str. 6/6—22/7/37.**G.**
Condensing gear removed.
Str. 18/3—10/5/39.**G.**
Str. 14/4—24/5/41.**G.**
Str. 14/9—11/11/43.**G.**
Str. 22/1—9/2/46.**G.**
Str. 22/8—20/10/48.**G.**
Str. 14—22/10/49.**C/L.**
Str. 26/6—17/8/51.**G.**
Str. 28/9—18/11/53.**C/L.**
Str. 21/6—7/8/54.**G.**
Str. 26/7—25/8/56.**C/L.**
Str. 2/1—2/2/57.**G.**
Str. 21/8—9/10/59.**G.**

BOILERS:
2079.
2061 10/3/33.
2081 5/7/35.
2071 22/7/37.
2072 10/5/39.
2075 24/5/41.
2067 11/11/43.
1945 9/2/46.
1941 20/10/48.
29034 17/8/51.
29054 7/8/54.
29110 2/2/57.
29046 9/10/59.

SHEDS:
Ardsley.
Stratford 3/9/28.

RENUMBERED:
9725 15/11/46.

69725 16/10/48.

CONDEMNED: 16/9/62.
Cut up at Stratford.

_____

2624

Doncaster 1696.

To traffic 27/9/28.

REPAIRS:
Str. 13/9—14/11/30.**G.**
Str. 19/12/32—7/2/33.**G.**
Str. 3/4—7/6/35.**G.**
Str. 17/3—7/5/37.**G.**
Condensing gear removed.
Str. 28/3—13/5/39.**G.**
Str. 28/5—30/6/41.**G.**
Str. 8/1—10/2/44.**G.**
Str. 23/1—9/3/45.**G.**
Str. 16/6—21/8/46.**G.**
Str. 30/12/48—5/3/49.**G.**
Str. 28/1—23/2/52.**G.**
Str. 13/5—25/6/55.**G.**
Str. 25/10—10/11/56.**C/L.**
Str. 6/8—12/9/58.**G.**
Str. 29/6—14/8/59.**C/L.**
Str. 5—25/2/60.**N/C.**

BOILERS:
2077.
2075 7/2/33.
2079 7/6/35.
2080 7/5/37.
2060 13/5/39.
1959 30/6/41.
1982 10/2/44.
2076 9/3/45.
1909 21/8/46.
1970 5/3/49.
29058 23/2/52.
29022 25/6/55.
29124 12/9/58.

SHEDS:
Ardsley.
Stratford 28/11/28.
Colchester 4/6/50.
Stratford 18/3/51.

RENUMBERED:
9726 23/11/46.
69726 5/3/49.

CONDEMNED: 4/12/60.
Cut up at Stratford.

_____

2625

Doncaster 1697.

To traffic 28/9/28.

REPAIRS:
Str. 1/11—23/1/31.**G.**
Str. 6/3—2/5/33.**G.**
Str. 1/5—5/735.**G.**
Str. 20/5—24/6/37.**G.**
Condensing gear removed.
Str. 22/4—8/6/39.**G.**
Str. 22/6—8/8/41.**G.**
Str. 20/2—31/3/44.**G.**
Str. 5/5—18/6/46.**G.**
Str. 19/12/48—1/2/49.**G.**
Str. 14/10—17/11/51.**G.**
Str. 28/3—30/4/55.**G.**
Str. 9/1—10/3/56.**C/L.**
Str. 24/8—15/9/56.**C/L.**
Str. 25/9—31/10/58.**G.**

BOILERS:
2080.
2055 2/5/33.
2076 5/7/35.
2058 24/6/37.
2073 8/6/39.
1951 8/8/41.
1985 31/3/44.
1955 18/6/46.
1958 1/2/49
29006 17/11/51.
29099 *(new)* 30/4/55.
29022 31/10/58.

SHEDS:
Ardsley.
Stratford 15/11/28.
Boston 2/12/49.
Stratford 14/5/50.
Parkeston 28/10/56.
Colchester 3/2/57.
Stratford 10/5/59.

RENUMBERED:
9727 21/10/46.
69727 29/1/49.

CONDEMNED: 24/11/60.
Cut up at Stratford.

_____

2626

Doncaster 1698.

To traffic 12/10/28.

REPAIRS:
Str. 24/1—2/4/31.**G.**
Str. 12/6—14/7/33.**G.**
Str. 30/11/34—25/1/35.**G.**
Str. 27/1—5/3/37.**G.**
Condensing gear removed.
Str. 14—26/5/37.**L.**
Str. 27/10—19/12/38.**G.**
Str. 26/11/40—3/1/41.**G.**
Str. 24/10—3/12/43.**G.**
Str. 16/9—7/10/44.**G.**
Str. 20/1—16/2/46.**G.**
Str. 29/8—17/10/48.**G.**

Str. 24—26/10/48.**N/C.**
Str. 23/3—27/4/50.**C/L.**
Str. 16/11—15/12/51.**G.**
Str. 27/5—22/7/55.**G.**
Str. 12—24/11/56.**N/C.**
Str. 31/3—1/5/59.**G.**
Str. 12—14/5/59.**N/C.**
Str. 24/11—17/12/60.**N/C.**

BOILERS:
2081.
2080 14/7/33.
2073 25/1/35.
2057 5/3/37.
2084 19/12/38.
2071 3/1/41.
1975 3/12/43.
1947 16/2/46.
1946 17/10/48.
29051 15/12/51.
29050 22/7/55.
29089 1/5/59.

SHEDS:
Ardsley.
Stratford 28/11/28.

RENUMBERED:
9728 19/9/46.
69728 16/10/48.

CONDEMNED: 10/9/61.
Cut up at Stratford.

_____

2627

Doncaster 1699.

To traffic 26/10/28.

REPAIRS:
Str. 24/9—15/11/29.**L.**
Str. 17/1—27/3/31.**G.**
Str. 21/8—22/9/33.**G.**
Str. 17/4—13/6/35.**G.**
Str. 1—10/11/36.**L.**
Str. 16/6—17/7/37.**G.**
Condensing gear removed.
Str. 6/8—22/9/39.**G.**
Str. 21/11—22/12/41.**G.**
Str. 25/6—12/8/44.**G.**
Str. 22/1—27/2/46.**G.**
Str. 20/6—13/8/49.**G.**
Str. 13/6—9/8/52.**G.**
Str. 6—27/4/54.**C/L.**
Str. 25/10—5/11/54.**C/L.**
Str. 8/6—12/8/55.**G.**
Str. 21/1—10/3/56.**C/L.**
Str. 27/8—10/9/57.**C/L.**
Str. 9/4—15/5/59.**G.**
Str. 27—31/7/59.**C/L.**

BOILERS:
2082.
2081 22/9/33.
2075 13/6/35.
2076 17/7/37.
2069 22/9/39.
2059 22/12/41.
1954 12/8/44.

No.69697 got the correct version of the BR crest when ex-works 27th November 1959 and was one of the seven withdrawn on 16th September 1962 when GE Section steam services ceased, and Class N7 became extinct.

2627 cont./
1949 27/2/46.
1913 13/8/49.
29117 *(new)* 9/8/52.
29063 12/8/55.
29099 15/5/59.

SHEDS:
Ardsley.
Stratford 18/4/29.

RENUMBERED:
9729 19/9/46.
69729 13/8/49.

CONDEMNED: 4/12/60.
Cut up at Stratford.

_____

2628

Doncaster 1701.

To traffic 15/11/28.

REPAIRS:
Str. 13/9—14/11/30.**G.**
Str. 16/3—4/5/33.**G.**
Str. 24/4—3/7/35.**G.**
Str. 27/6—24/7/37.**G.**
Condensing gear removed.
Str. 11/5—28/6/39.**G.**
Str. 13/6—8/8/41.**G.**
Str. 22/4—20/5/44.**G.**
Str. 13/10—29/11/46.**G.**
Str. 27/2—8/4/49.**G.**
Str. 12/6—28/7/50.**C/L.**
Str. 22/5—26/6/52.**G.**
Str. 22/5—21/7/56.**G.**
Str. 30/6—3/7/58.**C/L.**
Str. 16/6—7/8/59.**G.**

BOILERS:
2083.
2076 4/5/33.
2077 3/7/35.
2069 24/7/37.
2079 28/6/39.
2072 8/8/41.
1951 20/5/44.
1956 29/11/46.
1972 8/4/49.
29116 *(new)* 26/6/52.
29067 21/7/56.
29048 7/8/59.

SHEDS:
Ardsley.
Stratford 10/12/28.
Parkeston 29/11/59.
Stratford 24/1/60.
Parkeston 24/7/60.
Stratford 16/10/60.

RENUMBERED:
9730 21/9/46.
69730 8/4/49.

CONDEMNED: 10/9/61.
Cut up at Stratford.

_____

2629

Doncaster 1702.

To traffic 28/11/28.

REPAIRS:
Str. 30/5—8/8/31.**G.**
Str. 1/8—8/9/33.**G.**
Str. 8/6—26/7/35.**G.**
Str. 16/6—21/7/37.**G.**
Condensing gear removed.
Str. 3/5—16/6/39.**G.**
Str. 21/3—8/5/41.**G.**
Str. 13/2—11/3/44.**G.**
Str. 15/7—27/8/46.**G.**
Str. 15/5—18/6/49.**G.**
Str. 15—23/11/49.**C/L.**
Str. 23/7—6/9/52.**G.**
Str. 3/6—30/7/55.**G.**
Str. 1—20/11/56.**C/L.**
Str. 10—18/12/57.**C/L.**

BOILERS:
2084.
2085 8/9/33.
2068 26/7/35.
2055 21/7/37.
2063 16/6/39.
1955 8/5/41.
1981 11/3/44.
1985 27/8/46.
1953 18/6/49.
29076 6/9/52.
29058 30/7/55.

SHEDS:
Ardsley.
Stratford 26/12/28.

RENUMBERED:
9731 23/8/46.
69731 18/6/49.

CONDEMNED: 3/2/59.
Cut up at Stratford.

_____

2630

Doncaster 1704.

To traffic 20/12/28.

REPAIRS:
Str. 6/12—30/1/31.**G.**
Str. 22/5—29/6/33.**G.**
Str. 18/5—29/7/35.**G.**
Str. 22/8—3/9/36.**L.**
Str. 23/6—26/7/37.**G.**
Condensing gear removed.
Str. 2/8—16/9/39.**G.**
Str. 23/11/41—2/1/42.**G.**
Str. 3—7/2/42.**L.**
Str. 25/7—14/9/44.**G.**
Str. 14/9—4/11/47.**G.**
Str. 2/11—3/12/49.**G.**
Str. 29/8—9/10/52.**G.**
Str. 4/11/54—7/1/55.**C/L.**
Str. 6/1—18/2/56.**G.**
Str. 3—17/6/57.**C/L.**
Str. 1/7—28/8/59.**G.**

BOILERS:
2085.
2083 29/6/33.
2065 29/7/35.
2070 26/7/37.
2055 26/9/39.
2063 2/1/42
2057 14/9/44.
2063 4/11/47.
1983 3/12/49
29079 9/10/52.
29128 18/2/56.
29003 28/8/59

SHEDS:
Ardsley.
Stratford 28/1/29.
Colchester 15/11/53.
Parkeston 1/11/59.
Stratford 24/1/60.

RENUMBERED:
9732 22/11/46.
69732 3/12/49.

CONDEMNED: 10/9/61.
Cut up at Stratford.

_____

2631

Doncaster 1706.

To traffic 31/12/28.

REPAIRS:
Don. 11/1—12/2/29.**L.**
Str. 2/7—21/8/31.**G.**
Str. 11/9—10/10/33.**G.**
Str. 13/4—10/7/34.**H.**
Str. 17/10—12/11/35.**G.**
Str. 19/7—27/8/37.**G.**
Condensing gear removed.

Str. 16/7—25/8/39.**G.**
Str. 6/10—11/11/41.**G.**
Str. 29/4—9/6/44.**G.**
Str. 27/12/46—30/1/47.**G.**
Str. 3/6—23/7/49.**G.**
Str. 11—27/10/51.**C/L.**
Str. 16—26/1/52.**C/L.**
Str. 2/9—25/10/52.**G.**
Str. 22/4—27/5/54.**C/L.**
Str. 20/3—28/4/56.**G.**
Str. 28/5—25/6/58.**C/L.**
Str. 20/8—9/10/59.**G.**
Str. 6/10/60. *Not repaired.*

BOILERS:
2086.
2084 10/10/33.
2083 12/11/35.
2081 27/8/37.
2066 25/8/39.
1956 11/11/41.
2073 9/6/44.
2072 30/1/47.
1905 23/7/49.
1905 reno.29048 27/10/51.
29026 28/4/56.
24804 9/10/59.

SHEDS:
Ardsley.
Stratford 10/4/29.
Parkeston 28/10/56.
Colchester 3/2/57.
Stratford 1/11/59.

RENUMBERED:
9733 22/9/46.
69733 23/7/49.

CONDEMNED: 17/10/60.
Cut up at Stratford.

_____